THE MYSTERY OF ARTHUR AT TINTAGEL

THE MYSTERY OF ARTHUR AT TINTAGEL

An Esoteric Study

RICHARD SEDDON

RUDOLF STEINER PRESS

Rudolf Steiner Press
Hillside House, The Square
Forest Row, RH18 5ES

www.rudolfsteinerpress.com

Published by Rudolf Steiner Press 2013

First published in 1990. Reprinted 2013
© Richard Seddon 1990

A catalogue record for this book is available from the British Library

ISBN 978 1 85584 388 2

Cover by Andrew Morgan Design
Typeset by Emset, London
Printed and bound in Great Britain by 4edge Ltd, Essex

Contents

PREFACE

In an article concerning the Matter of Arthur, Rachel Bromwich—a leading modern scholar—saw fit to quote[1] a remark of Thomas Jones that, 'The first thing it is necessary to say is that there remains some mystery, some "magic meaning", in the great mystery which lies behind the whole.' Such a mystery, however, goes beyond the field of Celtic studies into that of metaphysics and spiritual science. The author, to his regret, has no knowledge of Welsh and no training in Celtic studies, and acknowledges with gratitude his debt to scholars, both living and deceased, for their translations and critical comments. But he does bring to the penetration of the underlying mystery both a qualification in Moral Sciences and forty years study of Anthroposophy, the modern science of the spirit. His very independence from the currently-received views of Celtic specialists may facilitate fresh insights in this field.

The attempt is made to let the relevant facts and documents speak their own message, as far as possible. Enormous progress has been made in Welsh scholarship in recent decades, but the premise that Arthur was a sixth-century military leader has inevitably conditioned its interpretations. The central theme of the present study is, however, that 'Arthur' was a title given to the leader of a spiritual school over many centuries. It is from this aspect that Anthroposophy can assist by bringing fresh light to bear. Such a view makes more intelligible the clustering of many legends around his name.

It is assumed that the reader is, or is willing to become, familiar with the Arthurian stories in the *Mabinogion*, which are the foundation of our British heritage. The first translation by Lady Charlotte Guest (1839-1849) was taken from the *Red Book of Hergest* (c. 1375/1425), and includes an eighteenth century manuscript about Gwion and Taliesin, as well as detailed notes. A new, annotated translation by T. F. Ellis and

J. Lloyd was published in 1929. The earlier *White Book of Rhydderch (*text c. 1300/25) received a scholarly translation by G. & T. Jones in 1948, (now in Everyman), and is mainly used here. The Penguin edition by J. Ganz (1976) 'has not attempted to be entirely literal'. *The Mabinogi* by P. K. Ford (1977) includes the tale of Gwion and Taliesin from an earlier but less detailed source, but only one of the five Arthurian tales, that of 'Culhwch and Olwen'. A century earlier than the others, this tale (referred to as *Culhwch* in what follows) has been described as a 'cyfarwyddyd' or 'guidance of a seer'; and the attempt is made to display this aspect.

Special acknowledgment is due to the late A. C. L. Brown[2], whose method of work on the sequences in Celtic legends gave rise to the plan of Chapters 3 and 4. But it will become evident that without the rich life-work of Rudolf Steiner (1861-1925), the founder of Anthroposophy, a treatment of the subject such as this could not have been undertaken at all. The results of his spiritual research have now been validated, at least in part, in so many diverse fields that it can no longer be ignored by those who claim to be unprejudiced. The author must however retain full responsibility for the use made of extracts from this work torn from their original contexts.

Just as we expect different descriptions of a single landscape from a farmer, a painter or a geologist, so we should expect different descriptions of the supersensible world from different ages, peoples and individuals. The necessary stages of soul-spiritual development in that world can nevertheless be recognized behind the various images used. Moreover, as we expect a geologist's report to contain some specialized terms, so a few unfamiliar terms are needed to describe the supersensible world, although these are here kept to a minimum. In seeking to illuminate extant Arthurian sources by actual inner experiences related by Rudolf Steiner, some statements have perforce been made which can be fully justified only out of the whole substance of Anthroposophy. Hence a sound critical judgment would need, as in any other subject, to be based on adequate understanding of this. The two works of Steiner most immediately relevant, out of the 327 volumes in the German edition to date, are his lecture course given in Penmaenmawr in 1923 translated as *The Evolution of Consciousness*, and his book *Theosophy*, written in 1904[3]. As he said after visiting Tintagel, 'It is our task to rediscover in fullest, clearest knowledge those things that we can, so to speak, map out when we look back into past ages, when we excavate in history, so that we may once again find it possible to bring about a new art of healing, a deepened artistic life, and a penetrating spiritual knowledge in humanity.'

It may help those unfamiliar with Welsh names to say that emphasis is usually on the penultimate syllable. As a rough guide, vowels have continental values; except that *w* is like the *oo* in 'moon'; and *y* is like the *u* in 'cut' (but if a final syllable, like the *ee* in 'deer'). Consonants resemble the English, except that: *c* is always hard; *f* corresponds to to our v, *ff* to our f; *dd* represents our 'th' as in 'then'; *th* sounding as in 'thick'; and *ll* is aspirated on the right as 'hl', with tongue-tip on palate.

Warmest thanks are due to G. R. Isaac for correcting a number of solecisms relating to Welsh material in Chapters 2-5, and to Dr. M. Haycock for permission to adapt the results of her researches; to Cecil Reilly for providing the very fine photographs of Tintagel; to others who have helped to bring this study to fruition; and especially to my wife Mary, not only for suffering for a decade the consequences of my researching, but also for helping to clarify my drafts, and for her help in proof-reading.

This study can be no more than a first exploratory step, which may encourage others with an understanding of medieval Welsh and also of the modern path of spiritual development to penetrate more deeply into the spiritual content of the Arthurian mysteries.

Richard Seddon
Whitsun, 1989

CHAPTER ONE

TINTAGEL AND ITS PROBLEMS

1. The Island in Ancient Times

The heart leaps as we set out for the 'island' of Tintagel—there is something in its atmosphere which has little to do with Norman castles, but is concerned much more with ancient times, something that touches the poet in us more nearly than the archaeologist. This experience is shared by many of the thousands who flock to this isolated spot each year. Poets, writers and musicians are among those who over the centuries have felt and responded to the impulse, deep within the soul, to climb its many steps in search for clues to the very tenuous legendary connection with Arthur and his Round Table which draws one on. As Geoffrey Ashe put it:[1] 'As shaped by Tennyson, the legend could only decline into children's books, romantic little societies, the gift shops and pastiche Hall of Chivalry at Tintagel.' And yet the legend is still alive and healthy. Stimulated perhaps by archaeological research into sites which might have formed the stronghold of a sixth-century warrior chief, it seems as if it is beginning to find some physical justification.

And now the early history of Tintagel itself has, since a fire in 1983 which cleared a large part of the surface of the island, become an open question. In addition to the forty or so small rooms disclosed by C. A. Ralegh-Radford in his partial excavation of the 1930s,[2] which he described with great confidence as the very model of a monastery of the fifth-sixth centuries, traces of another one hundred foundations, some of them 'probably much earlier' have now been identified and await excavation. And the pottery on which he based his dating now forms only a small fraction of the several thousand pieces recovered—more than from all other sites in Britain and Ireland together for the period between 450 and 650 AD. Charles Thomas, in the current British Heritage guide,[3] finds the luxury implied by these pieces quite incompatible with a monastery, and tentatively suggests that the site must have been a royal seat of the sub-kings of Cornwall for a substantial period.

Whilst awaiting full excavation it seems an opportune moment to examine afresh the early remains in the whole area, and the earliest documents relating to Arthur, to see what context they provide.

The ancient approach to the headland probably led by the gentle slope from the plateau where the parish church stands isolated from the village, and a monolith once stood here as waymark. This is a good place for strong walkers to park the car on the cliff, but those who after climbing the island may wish to use the jeep service back to the village will be well advised to park close to the bookshop which forms its terminus. It is possible from there to join the former approach by branching left across a stone slab spanning the stream about half-way down.

This approach leads through the outer ward of the medieval castle, where the island comes into view. Until the thirteenth century these were still joined by a neck of land so narrow that, as Geoffrey of Monmouth put it at the time:[4] 'three armed soldiers could hold it against you, even if you stood there with the whole kingdom of Britain at your side'. This link reached the top of the island near the left end of the medieval curtain wall that we see behind the inner ward of the Norman castle. To reach this point today, we need to descend and reascend, pass through the Norman ruins and the arch beyond them, and then turn back sharp left behind the curtain wall.

On reaching the top we shall feel the inclination to open ourselves first of all to the immediate experience of nature around us. It is indeed magnificent. We stand amidst an interplay of rock and sea, air and light. One day a gale nearly sweeps us off our feet, churning the sea into great waves that drive against the rocks with explosions of spray and foam. Another day all is still, whilst gentle ripples spread out in fans, and the rock on which we stand is hot to the touch. Or perhaps clouds are scudding across the sky, shafts of light playing an ever-changing pattern between sky and sea, a rainbow lighting up and vanishing away. Yet again, clouds may descend to wrap us tightly around in mist, or open upon us torrents of rain or drifting snow. We feel immersed directly and to an intense degree in those elements which were the subject matter of an ancient science. Whoever lived and worked here, if he was at all aware of his environment, must have been deeply involved with them.

The earliest buildings identified in the original excavations are two of the larger rectangular rooms on the crest (site A). One, dated to the third-fourth centuries, is extant at the south end, and is distinguishable by the use of larger stones. The other is a mere foundation to the north, built over about 500 AD without having been cleared back, as if its very existence was then unknown. The 1935 Guide asserted that these rooms represent the dwelling and barn of an early farmstead; but imagine yourself on this crest in midwinter—would any farmer, let alone a pioneer erecting a rectangular stone building when round wooden ones were the norm, choose such an exposed site rather than one in the shelter below? Whoever built here must have had a particular reason for his choice, to justify making himself conspicuous to any passing raiders at sea.

About 500 AD the longest room running between the two, with a small annexe, was built in herring-bone masonry. The room at the south end then accumulated debris and seems to have been supplanted. All other buildings excavated in the 1930s are dated to the sixth-seventh centuries, and may have been part of a great expansion, probably coupled with change of use, or may simply have been replaced buildings of wood. The screes which might give a clue were not examined.

There is an unusually solid foundation of unknown date, conjectured to represent a tiny oratory 9ft. long, between the southern room and the east end of the Norman chapel; the imported granite altar-stone of the latter, which lacks the usual consecration cross, may have come from it. Alongside was a 5ft. square block which may well have been the base of an open-air altar—probably for use at festivals when there were too many people to enter the oratory; or perhaps because an outside altar was in regular use, as in a Greek temple. In the chapel were found fragments of a slate headstone marked with a Maltese cross. Nearby were four shallow graves devoid of bones.

Whilst exploring the headland towards the sea, we come upon a remarkable short 'tunnel' (Plate 1) of which the Guide said, 'clearance has offered no clue to its date or purpose'. It slopes downwards for about 20 yds. (19m.), of which a quarter is still covered. It is 5ft. (1.5m.) wide, with sides arching to the same height, and was finished with metal tools. It was dry (though now silting up) but hardly suited to storage, which would have been provided much more easily above ground, would be preferably flat, and would need only one entrance. Outside the lower end the meadow slopes like a funnel towards the sea, the peace and beauty of the spot suggesting that it might have been held particularly sacred. Its purpose sets the second problem of Tintagel.

The whole area consists of some 20 acres (8 hectares), of which about a third was never built on. The composition of the island differs from most of the locality in that it is the extremity of a volcanic formation in an area of Devonian and Carboniferous slate. There is one volcanic layer at sea level, and another, folded double above it whilst molten. Within the coarse volcanic aggregate are fragments of dark-grey lava containing small crystals of iron minerals, especially magnatite, so that the magnetic susceptibility is higher than elsewhere in the locality. Another remarkable feature is the supply of fresh water to a spring and two medieval wells, which does not run dry even during severe drought, and must flow under the sea bed.

The area of the Norman castle, being the most sheltered spot, is likely to have attracted early occupation, but was thoroughly cleared back by the Norman builders. An earlier site with characteristic masonry and pottery was indeed found there, but was 'not explored further'. The ditch and earthen bank on which the medieval curtain wall was built is dated around 500 AD. It could never have served a defensive purpose, which would have been achieved much more effectively at the narrow point of access, but may well have separated some spiritual or regal community from people using the landing-point of the small harbour.

Geoffrey of Monmouth, who wrote about 1136 when his patron's brother was building the castle, seems to have known the site, and mentions a previous castle here in Arthur's time (which he wrongly placed only a few centuries earlier). And a century later the author of *The High History of the Holy Grail* probably followed tradition when he wrote of 'a great hall next to the enclosure where the abysm is', in the time of Arthur.

On descending to the shore one may, if the tide is low enough, explore the cave under the island popularly known as 'Merlin's Cave' (Plate 2). It, too, is open at both ends, like the 'tunnel', and is washed by the tide. A striking feature is a ledge on the left, easily accessible and possibly artificial, where one is cut off from direct light, and could well have contemplated the sounds and movements of the sea.

Full analysis of the artefacts recently found is awaited, but they include wide, flat dishes of fine red ware from Carthage and Asia Minor, suitable for ritual purposes, some inscribed with a cross; fragments of metre-high jars which probably brought oil, raisins or wine from Tunisia; amphorae from the Aegean islands or Turkey; small handled jars from Byzantium; and pieces of glass typical of Egypt in the fourth-fifth centuries. There are three pieces of slate, bearing inscribed drawings, one of which is of particular interest because of the way in which two human figures are depicted (Fig. 1). The inner outline of both contains the facial features, and outer outlines rise to a point above the head like an aura. A human outline on a fragment of red ware is also thought to show the double outline. These pose a third problem.

2. The Wider Site

Rather more than a mile north of Tintagel village through Bossiney lies a small but very beautiful valley, bounded to the south by the waterfall of St Nectan's Kieve ('basin' in Cornish), and entering the sea by a narrow cleft. Its steep sides give it the name of Rocky Valley, and the shelter which it affords, with its thick woods amid a barren landscape, must have always made it attractive to inhabitants of the neighbourhood in times of peace.

The area of the waterfall is most easily reached from the car park marked 'Rocky Valley', at the crest after the road has descended sharply. But a more attractive approach is by a footpath from the minor road junction at Bossiney, and to the right of the houses at Halgabron. On descending the side of the wooded valley one is struck by the width of the path and its steady gradient, as though one were on an ancient processional way; it may be so, or this may be the work of miners seeking fabled treasure at the Kieve during the last century. The path crosses the stream to join the other from Trethevey, and continues alongside the stream until, in marked contrast, it clambers haphazardly to the opposite crest, where modern access to the foot of the waterfall is gained. This is a straight drop of 40ft., caught in a basin, from which it emerges through a hole rather more than man-sized, then falling another 10ft. to a shallow pool at its base (Plate 3). With the least breeze the spray drifts across the warm and sheltered vale, its dampness making the steep sides lush with vegetation. To the left a broad ledge extends between the waterfall and the descending path; again one has the impression that this is an artefact, as though it were some ceremonial platform. And the path below the ledge is again wide and graded, leading to a flat area of considerable size now washed by the stream.

Such a spot has inevitably attracted to itself a number of legends. One is concerned with the burial of St Nectan with his treasure in the basin. Nectan is a name of Irish origin (Neachtán), identified since classical times with the Welsh Nudd (pronounced 'Neath'), king of the underworld. If there is substance in the suggestion by Brown[5] that the cognate of Arthur in Irish literature is Nu-ardu Necht, the coincidence that a key site near 'Arthur's castle' is named Nectan is striking. Since two other places also claim to be the burial place of 'St Nectan', it may well be that the attachement of his name to the Kieve is a monkist rationalization of the older name. In that case his 'treasure', which the miners could not find, would be the treasure of the otherworld in this 'fairy glen'.

A local Guide[6] speaks of 'monk-like figures suddenly appearing and suddenly disappearing; weird, mocking laughter; chanting at night; music from invisible musicians—these are all serious claims.' Reports of this kind can no longer be dismissed out of hand. Indeed, choral music of female voices was recently heard at midday near the point where the path from Halgabron crosses the stream, by a professor of music and his wife known personally to the author.

There is a report by Snell[7] of another reputedly genuine local legend 'though its antiquity may well be doubted... We are asked to believe that the knights, standing with bowed heads in the Kieve, undertook to search for the holy vessel of the Last Supper... The king, standing on the bridge of rock above the torrent, watched his reverent followers in the stream below laving their brows in its waters, listening to the music of the fall, and full of the inspiration of the scene, making their solemn vows, and with a firm desire after righteousness setting forth upon the quest. To this very spot, too, if legend be true, the knights who had failed returned.' Did such things in fact take place?

If one returns by the path to Trethevey and turns right up the main road for 300 yards, a large recumbent stone which forms the parish boundary may be seen by a gateway. Named 'King Arthur's Quoit', it is thought to have once been the capstone of a dolmen, its supports long removed for local purposes.

A small car park on the Tintagel side of the valley serves a footpath past Trevillet mill towards the sea. Where this path crosses the stream for the second time may be found by some ruins two similar rock carvings, each about twelve inches in diameter. The site is warm and dry, sheltered by the deep ravine, and with fresh running water to hand it is easy to see why it may have attracted early man, although peoples at that time usually dwelled for safety either on hilltops or headlands such as Tintagel and Willapark. Even today foliage arches over the banks to form natural arbours. The slate of Rocky Valley is often spotted with small rusty bleds of weathered pyrite, its cleavages crossed by abundant quartz-filled tension gashes.

The two carvings are of the 'classical' labyrinth, that on the right being apparently a relatively modern copy. That on the left, more perfect in form, (Plate 4) may well date from 1500 BC, as the official notice suggests, although its line, too, looks to have been subsequently scored by an iron tool. It would thus have originated in the Bronze Age, along with the 'cup and ring' marks found throughout Britain and Europe. Its labyrinth pattern is found on a coin from Knossos dated to 1500 BC; but it is also very widespread, being found in Indonesia, India (where it is used as a threshold mark and birth charm), Russia, across Europe to Ireland, and even in North America. A stone bearing a very similar pattern, now housed at Boscastle, is said to have been used until quite recent times by witches seeking to induce a condition of trance and atavistic clairvoyance. In medieval times the same pattern was frequently cut in turf and used for processions and courtship games, and many examples called 'Troy Towns' still exist. These may have originated in a fertility ritual. But why was this pattern carved here as a finger-labyrinth?

Returning to Bossiney ('dwelling of the bold chief'), one passes at the road junction a typical motte and bailey of the eleventh century, where two members of parliament used to be elected—among them Sir Francis Drake. This is one of the innumerable places where the Round Table is reputed to be buried—not, as might be expected, on the island. The choice of site appears quite arbitrary, until one finds that it is exactly midway on a line from St Nectans Kieve to the entrance to the island, and also happens to bisect a line between St Piran's well at Trethevey and the holy well near Tintagel vicarage. (Incidentally there are many springs and wells in this area.) Such a choice of site seems to suggest the precision of the cairn builders of Bodmin Moor (see next section) and may be very ancient.

Condolden barrow marks the burial of a Bronze Age chieftain, and several tumuli from that time have escaped the plough—one near Dunderhole Point, five beyond Trebarwith, and one inland at Menadue. There is an Iron Age double-banked fort at Trenale Bury, and the fortifications at Barras Head and Willapark (between the island and Rocky Valley) are assigned to the third or second century BC, when the village fort at Tregear Rounds, further south, was occupied by a people called the Dunmonii. The island is sure to have been occupied at the same time in view of its superior facilities; and it appears probable that its occupants needed a garrison to protect their independence.

Two inscribed stones, dated about 252 and 324 AD, found at Trethevey and in Tintagel respectively, suggest a road by that time, perhaps leading to the tin mines further south that are otherwise cut off by the Camel. But no trace of actual Roman occupation has been found in the neighbourhood.

Tintagel churchyard was typical in shape (before its extension) of the enclosure of a fifth century saint, and as so often seems to occupy an older site. On the seaward side are remains of an earthwork which runs under, and thus pre-dates, the churchyard bank and wall. This is interpreted as a signal station to watch for coastal raiders, though the island would have given the more unobstructed view, and it may have served more as a lookout landwards to the south. On the village side of the church are five oval mounds, two of which were opened to reveal burials in slate graves at considerable depth. These 'seem neither prehistoric nor medieval and are perhaps rather special early Christian graves'.[3] Other slate-lined graves have been found in the churchyard extension.

The church itself is dedicated, in common with that of the adjoining parish of Minster to the north, to a saint 'Materiana' or 'Merthyr Iana' (shrine of Iana). It would surely be unusual for a church to have been founded so close to the island if, in fact, there was a monastery there as has been supposed.

3. Bodmin Moor

Of the 35 locations mentioned by Ashe[1] as having attached to them the name of Arthur—and there are many others—the vast majority are either megalithic constructs or rock features in mountainous areas, such as people of that time frequented. This fact cannot conceivably result from the activities of any sixth-century war chief; yet writers on Arthurian matters have consistently chosen to overlook that another explanation must be sought. This leads us to consider the nature of the megalithic features closest to Tintagel, namely those on Bodmin Moor, where the map shows King Arthur's Hall on King Arthur's Downs, and King Arthur's Bed near Twelve Men's Moor; Trethevy Quoit at Tremar and the capstone at Trethevey near Bossiney, too, are each sometimes known as King Arthur's Quoit, possibly due to confusion of the former name with the latter.

The 5½ ft. monolith, now recumbent, in Tintagel churchyard probably relates to an ancient trackway said[8] to have led via the high ground of Trenale Bury, Condolden ('holed stone land') and Waterpit Down towards the Moor. There, within a distance of 10-20 miles (16-32km.) from Tintagel, were built during the centuries immediately following 2400 BC, at least

12 stone circles and 88 hilltop cairns. The construction of cairns on this scale—each 15-25m. in diameter, 12-15m. high, and taking up to 60 man-years to build—is unique within megalithic culture, and gave Cornwall its Cornish name (Kernow).

O'Brien has established[9] that 28 of these cairns gave accurate sightlines from one or other of the circles to significant positions of sun- and moon-rise and set. No doubt other cairns related to other observation points destroyed over the centuries, or to the passage of specific stars used to identify the constellations; this is a matter for future research. The sun alignments establish not only midwinter, midsummer and the equinoxes, but also the ancient festivals of Beltane and Samhain (Mayday and All Souls) and the intervening quarters of Imbolc (1 Feb) and Lugnasad (1 Aug, Lammas). King Arthur's Hall is aligned almost exactly North-South. Furthermore, from the group of three circles named 'The Hurlers', cairns mark the positions of sunrise every day from 13-31 Oct, and then twice weekly as the sun moves more slowly, until early December. This not only gave all the information needed to regulate the agricultural and pastoral year and the religious festivals, but much more than would be needed for that purpose during the autumn. What other purpose did the cairns and circles serve?

O'Brien, who is also a Sumerian specialist, goes on to justify a surprising but significant connection between the founders of Chaldean civilization, the Annan-age or Sons of Anu, and the megalith-builders of Ireland, the Tuatha de Danaan or People of Anu, whose heroes include Man-annan and Bu-annan; and through them with the House of Don in Wales and the Dunmonii in Cornwall. From the supporting facts we may single out the Sumerian Lord Ugmash, who is recorded as taking observations of the movement of the sun, and whose name meant 'sun wisdom'. In Ireland we find 'Ogma of the Sun Countenance' or 'Sun Learning', who is also recorded as moving great stones. He was the Sun-god Ogmius of the continental Celts, where he was known as god of eloquence, skilled in dialectics and poetry, and inventor of the Ogham alphabet. In

Welsh he appears as Ugnach, who invites Taliesin to his dwelling and to 'wine which briskly sparkled'. In Cornwall he becomes Gogmagog, or Goemagot in Plymouth. We shall revert later to this connection with Chaldea.

We should also notice the polarity between the megalithic culture and its contemporary in Egypt. Whilst the latter was developing geometry, surveying and the measurement of space, Cornish culture was studying predominantly the measurement of time: men were beginning to orientate themselves within the sense-perceptible realms of earth and sky respectively. Other aspects of this polarity have been characterized by Teichman,[10] for example: in Egypt, accurately-cut cubic blocks form small rectangular chambers within impressive buildings, whilst here, large unhewn boulders are open to the vagaries of our climate on the open moor, often in circles; in Egypt, art is mainly visual and the prerogative of the priesthood, whilst here music, song and dance are accessible to all; man's aim in Egypt is to become a long-lived scribe, preserving knowledge in a centralized state, whilst here the hero is one who dies in battle between the many petty kings. Such facts point to the complementary nature of the two cultures, the polarities of contemplation and deed respectively.

The Greeks regarded the mystery of time as that of Cronos (Saturn), who was the youngest of the seven Titans, rulers of the planets. Cronos killed and succeeded his father Uranos, but was in turn deposed by Zeus with the help of the Cyclopes, and banished with the other Titans to an island in the farthest west. Plutarch (AD 46-119) reports 'a land in the far west where every 30 years (the period of revolution of Saturn) the mysteries of Cronos were celebrated, when he was put to sleep in a rocky cave, bound by chains of gold'.

No residential teaching centre has yet been found on Bodmin Moor—the enigmatic enclosure 45 x 15m known as 'Arthur's Hall' can hardly have been more than a point of assembly for those working on the moor, if it is not a later construct by people living in the hut circles. It seems possible that Tintagel, within a day's walk and having advantages of defensibility and a position on the main highway—the sea—might have met this need. Its cave is nearer than any other to the moor.

4. 'Tintagel' and 'Celliwig'

The name Tintagel, which belongs properly only to the island (the present village having originally been called 'Trevena', 'the farm on the hill'), is itself problematic. It does not appear in the Domesday Book, and is first known from Geoffrey of Monmouth[4] in 1136, various manuscripts reading Tintagol, Tingagol, Tintgaol. If the name be of Cornish origin, Gover[8] suggests derivation from 'din', a stronghold (though elsewhere the 'd' is retained), and Breton 'tagell', a noose, referring to the shape of the headland; whilst Padel[8] translates this as a place where two waters meet (which they did not, so long as the promontory was intact up to the twelfth century). But there was no soft 'g' in Cornish at that date, and it is probably Norman-French. Jenner[11] suggested comparison with a rock on Sark called 'Tente d'Agel', said locally to mean 'castle of the devil'. Canner[8] has connected this with the biblical Azazel, who was regarded as a fallen angel and scapegoat; but the name is closer to that of the Hebrew Azael, who gives men the yearning for higher spirituality. No other possibility has yet been suggested.

Other pre-Norman religious foundations in Cornwall were never abandoned, and retained their original names, those with secular names pre-dating those named after a founder. But the island does seem to have been deserted between the ninth and the twelfth centuries; and Thomas has argued[12] that the original name, which had been lost, was in fact 'Rosnant', referred to in Irish annals as an important teaching centre lying south-east of Ireland. Meaning 'the large promontory by the valley', this well describes the island and Rocky Valley taken together. It would follow that 'Tintagel' was indeed Norman, and those who gave the name may have wished to show some disapproval of its previous reputation.

The dedication of the chapel on the headland does not help. It is known only from William of Worcester in 1478, and Leland in 1540, who wrote of 'a pretty chapel with a tumbe on the left side, dedicated to St Ulette alias Uliane'. Both Julitta and Juliana are among virgins invoked in a psalter from Rheims, probably written about 900 for Breton clerks taking refuge in Cornwall. Juliana was reputedly a sister of Nectan, whilst Julitta was a fourth-century Diocletian martyr, who was compelled to witness the dashing-out of the brains of her three-year-old child, and when beheaded thanked God that her child could never be taken from her again. These names may have been substituted for that of the Celtic St Juliot whose foundation is at Lanteglos—one could imagine a refugee cleric thinking them more apt for a shrine he heard had been forcibly closed.

Nothing here points to Arthur, who according to all early Welsh sources had his centre at Celliwig in Cornwall. According to Triad 1[13] Celliwig was one of his three 'tribal thrones', where Bytwini was chief bishop and Caradawg Strong Arm was chief elder; and in Triad 54 it is the scene of Medrawt's assault on Gwenhwyvar whilst Arthur was absent fighting against Rome.

Gwynn-Jones[14] has drawn attention to the work of several twelfth-century bards who wrote of Celliwig, not as a stronghold (caer) but as a centre of culture, which they supposed to be Tintagel. Thus Meuric ap Ierwerth wrote of 'Sovereign Arthur, whose temple shone with gold—he at Celliwig whose court was the noble cell of the muse'. And Cynndelw wrote that 'songs flowed as formerly at Celliwig' and of 'minstrels, as long ago they went to the court of Celliwig, to him who is the glory of men'. The *Stanzas of the Graves* refer to Llacheu, son of Arthur, 'whose arts were marvellous'.

The usual assertions that Celliwig was a fortified hilltop camp (caer) such as Killibury Rounds, 10 miles SE of Tintagel; Celliwith, NE of Bodmin, 13 miles away; or Callington, between Launceston and Plymouth, 25 miles away, may consequently be called into question. The name is said to derive from

'celli', a small wood or grove, and 'gwig', a wood or forest—
somewhat tautologous. Now a common title of the Deity was
'Celi Duw', corrupted from the Latin 'coeli deus'. 'Celliwig'
might therefore be taken to mean 'forest grove' with an over-
tone of divinity. One could not possibly find anywhere that
was more of a divine grove than St Nectan's Glen in Rocky
Valley.

Reports of Arthur's death lend mild support. The *Annales
Cambriae*, written down about 900 on the basis of older lists,
say that Arthur and Mordred received fatal wounds 'At the
strife of Camblan' about 540. And Geoffrey of Monmouth,[4]
using an unknown source, with names Cornish in form, pictures Arthur on his way home to Cornwall when he reached
Camblan. (Had the name derived from Camboglanna on the
Scottish border, the Welsh orthography would have retained
the 'g'.) A very specific story recorded before 1871[15] claimed
that Arthur was wounded by Mordred with a poisoned spear
in front of Worthyvale House on the Camel, and killed the latter at Slaughterbridge (which is however more likely to be
named from Old English 'slohtre', a marsh). The claim of
Glastonbury to contain Arthur's grave has been shown pretty
conclusively[16] to be a late invention derived from Gerald of
Wales—the *de Antiquitate Glastoniensis* by William of
Malmesbury (c. 1250) confirms that Arthur was mortally
wounded by Mordred 'near the river Camba in Cornwall', and
that his grave was unknown.

A problem of a different kind is posed by a passage quoted
by Newstead[17] from the medieval *La Folie Tristan d'Oxford*:
'If of old you were to call Tintagel the faery castle, this 'faery
castle' would be rightly spoken. For twice a year it vanishes.
The peasants truly said that twice a year it could not be seen
by anyone in the district, not by anyone at all, however great
attention they paid—once in winter and once in summer—so
local folk say'. However improbable such a statement may at
first seem, what lies behind it will need to be further considered
in Chapter 4.1.

The foregoing certainly does not prove anything, but taken

together it does lend support to the idea that Celliwig was Tintagel/Rocky Valley, and that it was once the centre of spiritual activity in the name of Arthur. What it became during the expansion of the sixth century is beyond our present scope.

This does not of course preclude the possibility that there was also another 'Arthur' in the Old Welsh North in the sixth century, who was the warrior referred to in the Gododdin ('he glutted black ravens on the fortress wall, though he was no Arthur') and in the *Marwnad Cynddylan* ('the stout whelps of Arthur'). But the main tradition points clearly to Cornwall, most probably Tintagel, as the base of 'Arthur'.

CHAPTER TWO

THE OTHERWORLD DIMENSION

1. Tintagel as Mystery Centre

It has always been known that civilizations of the past received their impulses from mystery centres, which were at the same time centres of wisdom, art and religion. In the age of classical Greece, for example, there were such centres at Delphi, Eleusis, Samothrace, Epidauros, Ephesus and elsewhere.[1] There were similar centres, though different in substance, in the north-west of Europe, such as New Grange in Ireland and the Externsteine near Paderborn. The thesis will be here advanced that Tintagel was such a centre for the Arthurian mysteries.

The task of a mystery centre was to cultivate a particular training of soul and spirit in a way that would give generations of pupils a direct experience of the supersensible forces and beings active in the creation of the world and man, and to reawaken the folk memory of the stages by which human consciousness had evolved, so as to guide it wisely into the future. It was thus a repository of wisdom concerning the starry worlds, the nature of the human being not only during his life on earth but also between death and rebirth, the healing qualities of plant and mineral substances, and the crafts of practical life. Each centre approached such questions from an aspect which differed according to its geographical environment and the propitiousness of this for unfolding the specific forces to be used in training; and it was necessary for the high initiates to travel to different centres in search of a wholeness of experience. The wisdom itself was kept as a closely guarded secret, granted only to those who had shown themselves by rigorous tests to be fit to carry the responsibility, and unwarranted disclosure was punishable by death. Only a small fragment of the content was translated into ritual and legend for the education of the general populace, and hence a study of what has come down to us, often in degenerate form, can only lead to the fringe of the subject. Only spiritual research based on exact method such as that of Rudolf Steiner—likely to become increasingly widespread in future as his methods are practised—can provide the context for the full understanding of such fragments. A new dimension has thus been added to investigations into the distant past.

Steiner has written and spoken in considerable detail about the evolution of human consciousness in successive ages in different parts of the world. The particular task of the Arthurian mysteries was, he said,[2] to carry certain secrets of Egyptian-Chaldean times (contemporary with the constructs of Bodmin Moor) into the Christian age. These were secrets connected with the inpouring of the forces of the zodiac and planets, particularly the way in which the influences of sun and moon vary as they pass round the zodiac. 'Those forces inspired certain people—not exactly through their training, but through certain mystery influences—as their instruments. Into the twelve knights of the Round Table flowed the inspirations from the zodiac; they were surrounded by others representing the starry host, into whom flowed inspirations more distantly distributed in cosmic space; the inspirations from the spiritual forces of sun and moon were represented by Arthur and Gwenhwyvar (Guinevere). Thus we find the cosmos humanized . . . The inner mysteries taking place in souls refining and purifying the forces of the astral body were expressed in pictures as the slaying of monsters, giants and the like.' This transmission of wisdom from a previous age gives the first plausible answer to the question why the name of Arthur is attached to so many megalithic sites.

Rudolf Steiner visited Tintagel on 17 Aug 1924, during a conference at Torquay in the last year of his life. His biographer, G. Wachsmuth, who was present on this occasion, gave the following description:[3] 'He spoke there, standing on the cliff, about the experiences of the knights of King Arthur, who experienced in the eternal struggle here of forces of light with the elements of the earth a reflection of their own inner battles, where in the realm of soul and spirit light and darkness battle for mastery, and the ego force, the illuminated consciousness of man, strives in ceaseless battle to achieve mastery over the clouds of passions. He spoke of the teaching of Merlin which was fostered, of the service of the spiritual sun practised in Arthur's circle, and their knowledge of the cosmic deeds of Christ. As then on the highest point of the cliff he surveyed the remains of the walls of the medieval castle, which indicates the structure of the mystery place of King Arthur in its external lines, the past became present in his spiritual vision, and he described to us in living pictures—pointing with his hand to various parts of the castle—where the Hall of the Round Table had once been, the rooms of the king, and of his knights. The immediacy of the spiritual vision was so intense that during the description the entire reality, the extended life and action, the inner willing and achievement of the circle of King Arthur's knights, stood before us as actual experience. That such an occurrence is actually possible in our time—this fact gave to those hours on the cliff of Arthur's castle in Tintagel the sacred character of a deed which is inscribed in the annals of history.'

On his return to Torquay, and as he passed through London on his return journey, Steiner gave two lectures[4] which place his experiences at Tintagel within the context of the whole spiritual evolution of western Europe. These will be referred to in what follows. But it must be said at once that he experienced 'Arthur', not as a single person, but as a rank, held by successive leaders of the mystery school over many centuries. This again provides an intelligible answer to the question why so many legends, often of an otherworldly character, were formed around his name.

2. Pre-Celtic Mysteries

We need first to consider briefly the ancient times whose wisdom was to be transmitted. Four main stages in the evolution of consciousness can be traced in Welsh sources: a time before about 3100 BC, when people were aware as if in dream-pictures of their spiritual environment; a second extending in various phases until about 800 BC, when this awareness of forces of the starry worlds was lost to all except an initiated priesthood, whilst awareness grew of the world of nature and the elemental beings and forces at work in it; thirdly the great age of classical Greece, when the Arthurian mysteries flourished, and when sense-impressions increasingly predominated, but the otherworld was still for many a lively experience in imaginative pictures; and the last age, in which only sense-impressions remain, but it begins to be possible for a person to regain an inner experience of the elemental and starry worlds through individual effort.

A glimpse of the earliest period may be gained from the discovery at Star Carr in Yorkshire (radiocarbon 7500 bc) of 21 stag frontlets with antlers, perforated for attachment to headdresses. By radiating the forces by which a stag creates its antlers, a stag lives strongly in its environment, and absorbs the forces of the starry world which works organically into its nerves and senses, suffusing it with a gentle nervousness. This was also the ideal of ancient human consciousness at that time, later expressed in worship of the antlered god Cernunnos depicted on the Gundestrup cauldron, and still remembered in the horn-dance. Even before Britain became an island (6000 bc) hunter-gatherers were using fire and bow, and engaged in decorative art. Later in this period we find substantial forest clearance, communal farming, and quite large houses up to 50 x 25ft.[5] Several thousand tombs survive—rotunda graves with central cist in Gloucestershire, portal dolmens in the West, simple passage graves in North Wales and Scotland, mortuary areas fronted by a facade in East and South; and from 2800 bc long barrows, each taking ten men up to six months to amass. Proper preparation for continued life in the environment after death was clearly of great importance to these peoples.

About 3100 BC (2500 bc) a crisis occurred. Enclosures were deserted, and scrub and woodland regenerated on land previously cleared. The long-skulled people virtually disappeared, to be replaced by the round-skulled people of later times, the builders of the round barrows. Vessels were of a coarser Peterborough ware, flint and bone working was cruder; and all over the country the entrances of the older monumental tombs were blocked. Instead, henges and larger stone circles such as Stonehenge, and other constructs showing a concern for celestial movements, began to be built. What had happened?

We face here an inherent problem in data. It is well known that all ancient mysteries kept their wisdom secret on pain of death. When, however, a tradition dies out, remnants may well be disclosed. Edward Williams (Iolo Morganwg) claimed to have received such a source, which he published in the middle of the last century; but his character was such that his claims—which are, *ipso facto*, unsupported by earlier texts—are very much open to doubt. Virtually all we have concerning the god Hu unfortunately comes from this source. We can but judge intuitively from its content whether each item is fabricated or genuine.

Such a questionable but plausible source tells how 'the abyss of waters broke out', until Hu harnessed his twelve oxen (who bellow in thunder and glare in lightning) and 'drew the Avanc out of the flood, thereby stopping the inundation'. Dwyvan and Dwyvach (male and female) alone were rescued in a ship built by Hu which had no sails. This closely resembles the story of Noah, and others of similar date. These cannot refer back to physical floods at the end of the Ice Age, or even to the separation of Britain from the Continent and Ireland, which were much earlier (and not due to an Avanc!). In Greece it was known as the Deu-kalion flood, and in Indian tradition as the beginning of Kali Yuga, the Dark Age. Steiner says of this:[6] 'In the case of many human beings it came about that for a time all (spiritual) vision departed from them, and darkness spread over their souls. This condition of darkness did not last for long periods, actually only for weeks. But men passed into this condition, and many never came out of it. Many of them perished, and only relatively few were left, in widely scattered regions. . . This condition of sleep was felt by most souls as a kind of 'drowning', and only by a few as a reawakening. And then came the Dark Age, the age devoid of the Gods.'

What then was the Avanc, the monster drawn out of this flood by Hu? It was the experience of the sense-perceptible world of nature, newly irradiated by the sun (huan). And it occurred when he yoked his oxen, namely at the beginning of the Taurean Age, 3100 BC. Hu is the sun-power who penetrated the cloudbanks, so that the world of objects lit by the sun predominated in human consciousness, and men saw the rainbow. Hence there is a certain inner truth in the Welsh tradition recorded by Nennius and followed by Geoffrey— seeming to us so improbable—which derives the 'History of the Britons' from one of the sons of Noah. The former questionable source adds that Hu the Mighty conducted the Cymry (comrades) from the Summer Country 'where Constantinople now stands' to Britain, ruling them with justice and peace, and tamed the ox that draws the plough. In the ox or cow the starry forces of the cosmos work right down into the metabolic process, and it is this that lies behind the well-established cult of the bull. That such a cult continued to exist in Wales receives support from the fact that Triad 6 refers to 'The Three Bull Protectors', Triad 7 to 'Three Bull Chieftains' and Triad 63 to 'Three Bull Spectres'.

It is hard to imagine what human consciousness was then like, and in view of the connection we saw (Chapter 1.3) between Cornwall and Chaldea it is interesting that Steiner spoke a week before he went to Tintagel[7] of what the Chaldeans experienced. By day they saw objects, but still blurred as in a fog, with a spiritual essence raying out like spray. But by night they still had mighty pictures in flowing tides of colour, from which arose strange demonic forms, together conceived as a great dragon; they saw the goddess Ea (the Greek Soph-ia, all-permeating wisdom) sending to mankind her son Merodach/Marduk, 'the young bull of the sun' (in Hebrew terminology Michael, the leading Archangel); and they saw how with the force of his storm-wind he burst asunder the dragon, forming the shining heavens above and the growing things of earth below. This is another picture of the same change in consciousness as that of Hu and the Avanc.

Both the Chaldean and the Arthurian mysteries felt that their task was to draw forth from their feeling of the spirit weaving in the stars all that was needed for practical and social life. The configurations and movements of the stars were read particularly by the Chaldeans as a real astrology which revealed man's life between death and rebirth, of which they still had a clear perception. Davies[8] long ago quoted Anton Liberal (c. AD 20) as saying that Babylonians (Chaldeans) often visited the temple of Apollo in Hyperborea, and attempted to introduce its sacrifices into their own country. Even Hindus, he adds, visited these islands, which they regarded as 'the abode of the Pitris' or Fathers.

Reverting to Cornwall, a special characteristic of megalithic constructs there was the use of a circle rather than a single stone as the point of astronomical observation. Studies elsewhere[9] have shown that stone circles have remarkable qualities, even after 4000 years. These include ultrasonic silence; radioactivity often less than half that outside the circle; a seven-ring pattern detected electromagnetically; and seven rings detected by dowsing, but with a line or lines radiating from the centre (compare Plate 4). In view of the astronomical alignments on the moor, these characteristics are very unlikely to be natural features, but rather the consequence of repeated processional or cult movements related to the sun, moon and planets.

We can imagine a ceremony around 2000 BC at The Hurlers on Bodmin Moor each night during the autumn, when members of a local community are led by a priest in procession,

or perhaps watch priestesses in procession, into and around
one of the three circles, following some such pattern as that
carved in Rocky Valley, which we saw (Chapter 1:2) was connected with fertility and change of consciousness. The procession culminates in silence, awaiting dawn. The priest can
still perceive the sun clairvoyantly through the earth, greenish-
blue at the centre surrounded by a shining golden red, and
moving as if in a funnel,[7] and can predict behind which cairn
it will rise. Those who have lost the faculty to see this will
nevertheless see it when the sun stands behind the lesser
thickness of the cairn (there is a last remnant of this experience
in the otherwise unexplained 'green flash' sometimes seen at
the moment before sunrise). If the greenish-blue light of the
sun-god appears, the people feel blessed by him, and the
wisdom of the priest is vindicated; if not, they feel
admonished; and the priest, who sees individuals as dark
centres in a general auric cloud, perceives their moral response
in the change of this aura.

There was no brain able to think as ours does; wisdom was
received as revelation from the angelic world. But preparation
had to be made for the capacity to think, and Steiner has drawn
attention[10] to a pioneer of the bards, a superhuman
individuality comparable to Orpheus, who brought this about
by a special kind of music, full of enchantment. People felt
this music as a song from the realm of light, like the rising and
setting of an inner sun; for it took hold of the thought-
substance active in the process of vision (through which we
identify at once what we perceive) and raised it into consciousness. This enabled them to differentiate conceptually between the outer objects that were newly visible—the first step
towards logical thought. We can feel this connection between
music and thinking directly when we listen to the bell-ringing
of changes peculiar to Britain.

The originator and patron of bards, minstrels and musicians,
according to the Welsh bardic schools which flourished with
scarcely a break up to the seventeenth century, was called Bran.
A poem ascribed to Taliesin names Bran as bard, harper, crwth-

player and seven-score other musicians in one. In earliest times the bards, who felt themselves to be out of the body, looking back from cosmic heights and living in the music of the spheres, were the seers and prophets, representing the inward path of experience, and were superior to the druids, who possessed the outer practical wisdom; but in course of time the latter came to take precedence.

Traditions of this great teacher of the West were later gathered by the Greeks into their conception of Apollo with his lyre, who was said in the mysteries of Delphi to spend each winter (or once in nineteen years) in the region of Hyperborea. Indeed Pindar (520-440 BC) wrote: 'Apollo was worshipped by the Hyperboreans in the style of Osiris or Dionysius. Neither by ships nor by land can you find the way. In the shadow of cromlechs, priests read runes announcing the sun-spirit in air enwrapped by Helios.* Apollo rejoices; they make merry with dances of girls, lyres and flutes . . . A happy folk, aloof from labour and war.' Many are the folk-tales of stone circles as dancing maidens turned to stone, often with the hele stone as the fiddler.

An echo of this music of Bran may exist in a sixteenth century copy 'supposed to have been handed down to us by the British druids' from a congress of musicians known to have been held in 1040 AD. Arnold Dolmetsch said of this:[11] 'The only source of knowledge of polyphonic music of the pre-Christian civilizations is through our priceless Welsh manuscript . . . (It) contains harmonies not only fully developed according to modern ideas, but carried to fantastic heights of freedom and daring, without ceasing to be logical and convincing. This harmony existed, we do not know how many thousands of years ago . . . The music, so scientific in its inception, is actually simple and close to nature. Its spirituality speaks directly to the inner faculties of receptive listeners, and rouses their emotions to a degree far beyond the

---

* Helios (Welsh 'heul') personified physical sunlight, Apollo the spiritual sun forces of life and love working through the elements.

powers of ordinary music . . . In many ways, it is the finest and most profound music in the world . . . To me, this music is sacred.' It is sad that it is rarely heard.

There are several indications that Arthur was regarded as the successor to Bran, not musically but as leader on the inner path. The Irish *Voyages of Bran* describes an outer physical journey which is also an inward spiritual development. The tale of 'Branwen' in the *Mabinogion* tells how Bran the Blessed owned the cauldron of regeneration (he was master of the astral forces working from the stars during sleep). To save his sister he made an expedition to Ireland (the otherworld), wading there, because 'in those days the depth of water was not wide'. After the ensuing battle, on the Irish side, 'no one was left alive save five pregnant women', whilst on Bran's side only seven returned. We shall consider in Chapter 2.5 the report of an expedition of Arthur to the otherworld, also involving a cauldron, from which only seven returned, in both cases including Taliesin. Bran, poisoned in the foot, commanded that his own head be cut off, and it remained incorrupt and accompanied the seven for 87 years, until 'the door towards Cornwall' was opened. They were then required to bury the head on the White Hill in London, for 'no plague would ever come across the sea to this island as long as the head was in that concealment'. However a variant of Triad 37 reads: 'And Arthur uncovered the head of Bran the Blessed, because it did not seem right to him that this island should be defended by the strength of anyone but his own.' (Presumably before the Roman invasion!)

Two Irish texts refer to 'Arthuir son of Bran' and Artur brother of Bran' respectively. The name 'Bran means 'raven', the dark bird of omen and messenger of the gods; and Graves has shown[12] that the tree sacred to him was the alder, from the bark of which a red dye was produced. Is it mere coincidence that the only two farmsteads in Rocky Valley are named Halgabron (raven moor) and Trevillet (red farm)?

3. The Course of the Year

There were no large enclosed temples in north-west Europe, as there were in Egypt and Chaldea; the basis of initiation here was instead an enhanced experience of nature, as it came to expression in the ever-changing course of the year, so gentle compared with the harsh deserts of eastern cultures. This used to be experienced as a trinity: the polarity of summer and winter, and the intermediate stage of spring/autumn. The earth with all its plants and creatures was felt in its totality as a huge living organism, which breathed out its forces in summer and breathed them in again in winter. In the earliest times no attention was paid to the mineral kingdom, nor to the human form itself. The whole experience was much more intense and overpowering than we can imagine with our modern intellectual approach.[13]

In summer the earth, and man with it, was felt to be completely expanded in the warmth, exhaled into the cosmos. The insect world rose into the sun-laden air, and the buds of spring were transformed into many-coloured blossoms through the touch of the sun's rays, mirroring back in their multiplicity the manifold realm of the starry worlds. The very air and warmth were felt as themselves developing around midsummer something of a plant-like nature. It was a time of joyful exultation in the superabundant life of nature. And in midsummer festivals, questions were put to the powers of the cosmos in the form of music and song, with the help of simple instruments and rhythmical dances. Then the response of gods no longer visible was awaited, perhaps in the dramatic course of their midsummer night's dreams, or perhaps in the ensuing climate—thunder on a sultry day being taken as a moral admonition, the warm glow of a summer's eve as an enlightenment. Thus men felt united with the upper gods. On the other hand, the hard baked earth drew attention at this time to the earthly forces of hardening which they began to recognize as the mineral element, and found also in their dreams as the beginning of an inner consolidation, later becoming the ego.

In the seclusion of the mysteries the priests felt the need to express through sacrificial offerings at midsummer their gratitude to the gods by whom, up to the ninth century BC, they felt their thoughts to have been inspired. The leaders went to such ceremonies bearing the insignia of this wisdom, of which they ritually divested themselves one by one, really becoming ignorant again during August and September. Solemn words of prayer and thanksgiving were spoken into rising smoke, setting it into waves, and thus inscribing into the atmosphere their feelings of thanks for the thoughts that had been granted to them. Only the healers were allowed to retain their wisdom, but their sacrifice lay in being only servants of the mysteries.

In the stillness and quiet of midwinter, on the other hand, the attempt was made to strengthen by inner effort the reflective forces which made men sly and cunning—especially after the eighth century BC, when the feeling that they themselves produced their thoughts first began to arise. All manner of enigmas and riddles (themselves an otherwise puzzling characteristic of northern literature) were used, as well as such things as the throwing of runic wands. They felt as though their will was caught at this time in a frosty element of destruction and gloom rising from the earth up to their waist, as though their instincts and desires were steeped in gravity and other earth-forces—a real experience of death, polaric to the full life of summer. But as they felt their way towards an understanding of the processes of root and seed beneath the soil and snow, they came upon the sun forces of the previous year (which, for example, keep potatoes fresh in the clamp); and in the healing effect that enabled the roots to thrive they recognized the lower gods. By means of a primitive plastic art in all kinds of materials, including water as it froze, they learned how the earth's forces give shape to animal forms, and to the human form itself. This was an activity in which all, and not only the priests, took part.

Rudolf Steiner has described in remarkable detail how in the

Hibernian mysteries this polarity between summer and winter was developed in connection with male and female statues into an initiation experience of the greatest depth and significance;[14] but this lies outside our present scope. We may, however, note a heritage of nature poetry which attained written form in both Ireland and Wales from the ninth to the twelfth centuries, some two or three centuries earlier than elsewhere in Europe. Kenneth Jackson has said of this[15] that 'the curious irregular and unusual style, like adaptations of syllabic metres to an earlier nature rhetoric, suggests that the poet was deliberately archaizing, and therefore aware of an older tradition of seasonal poetry . . . The ultimate source may be no more than a general interest in the phenomena of the seasons, but the very definite genre seems to demand some more specific explanation.' We may also note that in the Celtic church, heaven was represented in terms of summer, fair weather, beauty and prosperity; whereas hell was not, as in the Roman church, a blazing inferno, but winter and snow, tempest, cold, old age, disease and death.

The British and Northern mysteries, however, took account also of the intermediate seasons. Spring was the time of hope. People were led to observe how forces from the earth shoot up into the plant, how in the buds the rounded or serrated leaf-forms differ in the sunlit meadow or in forest shade. They saw how the air is not only filled with insects but itself 'greens' (Goethe's phrase), and how the elemental beings dissolve, hover and soar away into the clouds as they fall into a condition of sleep. They felt how their own souls too were lost in sense-enjoyment and flowed out in the sunlight, so that they could no longer 'think about' the world; but how, on the other hand, through the reading of such 'letters' in the book of nature, they could experience the creative forces which shaped not only nature but also their own bodies.

On the other hand, as the mists of autumn drew on amid the colouring, withering and falling leaves, the ripening of fruits and the formation of seeds, the migration of birds and the hibernation of animals, a mood of sadness and melancholy prevailed. Men felt within themselves, however, a stirring of the intellect, and carried their active work into the dying nature in preparation for the year ahead.

A 'suspect' text (Chapter 2.2) tells, for example, how the death and burial of Hu were celebrated at an autumn festival. We hear of a solemn procession before a lake, with an ox, and an eagle carried aloft in the path of the sun, the 'splendid mover'. The chief druid Aeddon (cf. Adonis) was laid in the grave, and then carried across to 'black island', the land of the dead in the west: 'Disturbed is the island by the praise of Hu, the island of the severe rewarder, even Mona of the generous bowls which animate vigour.' Another song describes Hu as 'the prey of the depths', passing through nine stages under the guidance of the 'woman of beauty', namely his consort Ceridwen. There is reference to 'the long toil of the just ones, led by Hu and Aeddon, on the sea which has no shore'.[16] Then at a spring festival Hu 'rose again', his immortality signified by a sprig of ivy. This was the time when candidates for initiation were put through rigorous tests, and emulated Hu's rising from the dead through the new life forces coming from the sun.

By feeling the way deeply into the four seasons as they have been briefly sketched, it was possible to distinguish not only the course of the year, but also the fundamental concept of man himself that was found in the mysteries.[13] The spring reveals the visible process of physical growth and development throughout nature, which also gives man in childhood his physical, corporeal body. Summer reveals its abundant life-forces in the etherealization of scents, which are also active in the life-processes of man's etheric or life-body that continues up to the moment of death; these life forces are not present in the corpse, nor in the mineral kingdom, but man shares them with the plants and animals. The autumn process of withering and decay in nature works in man and animal all through the year, where it holds back the life-forces to allow a dreamy form of consciousness to arise; this is the astral body, which in man has two parts—one hereditary, and shared with the animal kingdom, which contains the lower instincts, desires and passions of an earthly nature; the other of a higher kind, the soul element, which has been purified by human culture through the ages, and remains more directly related to the stars. The winter experience of death in nature, coupled with a quickening of life underground, corresponds to the ego in man, the spiritual core awakened through individual effort, which is first experienced in reflection in the soul as self, and later becomes known in its inner reality through spiritual development as the selfless higher self of man. We shall come upon these four principles in many different forms in what follows.

It is clear that for a full understanding of man, including the manifold relationships between these four principles in each different organ of the body, experiences from the whole course of the year must be brought together into one. But the ego of that time united so intensely with nature that, had the attempt been made to unite it with the qualities of several seasons at once, this ego—despite its healthy elemental strength—would have become lost, like a drop in a lake. The initiator had therefore to bring support from outside through a team of helpers, who with intense devotion and self-sacrifice each placed all their forces of soul in just one season, and were willing to forgo deepening their own experience of the remainder.[17] Three such individuals were needed for each season, twelve in all, so that together they had a sufficient surplus of ego-force to transmit to the candidate. He could then experience the whole cycle of the year with balanced intensity. Here we find the origin of the so-called Round Table.

In this way it was made possible for the candidate who was properly prepared to rise at midsummer out into the cosmos, to experience the successive levels of the soul-spiritual world which lay beyond the visible world and gave rise to it, and afterwards to report to his helpers something of what he had experienced. First he gained a living experience of the craftsmen in the workshop of nature and in man's etheric body, the world of the elements centred in the moon-sphere. Next he experienced the higher world of spiritual beings directing this

workshop from the sun and planets as they moved around the
zodiac. They were felt in the starry or astral body, which is
the foundation of consciousness and the instrument of the
inspirations received through the twelve helpers. Through
these twelve constellations the human ego is formed within
the astral body. Finally he would come, if fully successful, to
the whole panoply of heaven, including the Milky Way,
whence flow the impulses of the supreme Deity, the holy
Trinity, source and origin of the universe. They give to man
his self-conscious awareness of his own eternal being or higher
self, its divine origin and goal. As we shall see, further divisions of these stages, such as the 'nine stages of Hu and
Ceridwen', were made.

4. The Age of the Celts

Around 1200 BC (1000 bc) the proto-Celts, named Urnfielders
because of their flat cremation cemeteries, began to reach Britain. The climate became colder and wetter, and they were
not, in any case, particularly interested in the starry world and
its beings. But they were acutely aware of the elemental beings
of nature around them, as is at once apparent from the beauty
of line in subsequent Celtic art. This necessitated the founding
of a new mystery school of a different kind. Is it mere coincidence that Geoffrey of Monmouth put the conquest of Britain
by Brutus from the giants at 1170 BC?

From the amount of fine metalwork, of a prestigious rather
than of a practical nature, found in rivers, lakes and bogs during
the period until Roman times, archaeologists have suspected
the existence of a water cult.[5] And the outstanding
characteristic of Tintagel, when compared with the other
mystery centres mentioned in Chapter 2.1, was always its relation to water. On the one hand the promontory projects into
and is almost surrounded by the sea; at its foot the waves burst
into spray or swirl around the cave, and from its summit is
a broad vista of storms across the sea. On the other hand at

St Nectan's Kieve the waterfall is received into the rocky cleft as if into the earth's womb, to flow on as murmuring stream. Nor is this all. Between the two are no less than nine springs, with another on the promontory itself—points where water flows upwards towards the sky like sense-organs of the earth. And there are surfaces of glassy stillness—wells on the promontory, near the vicarage, and at Trethevey, Bossiney pond, and Dozmary pool on the moor.

Since water is the bearer of life, of the etheric forces, we can understand Steiner's remark that the great question living in the Arthurian mysteries was how a pupil was to find his orientation in the etheric cosmos. This meant, of course, not just a study of the points of light visible in the night sky, but the very practical and vital question as to the nature of the path that must be taken by the human being in this cosmic ether, either in the passage from death to rebirth, or in the process of initiation by means of which this path was investigated. This reconciles, in an unexpected way, viewpoints such as that of A. Burl,[18] who in discussing Stonehenge emphasizes its role as a mortuary temple, and those who emphasize its astronomical orientations. It is the answer to this question, above all, which was contained in the legends to be examined in the ensuing chapters.

During the evening of his visit to Tintagel, Rudolf Steiner wrote a verse to the Swiss poet Albert Steffen which may be translated as follows:[19]

We come from castle ruins, eloquent.
Here dwelled the demon-conquerors of old,
Their leader's strength through zodiac enhanced.
The castles are in ruins,
The starry world grown dumb;
Yet spirit-power lies heavy round the mount,
And mighty images of soul storm from the sea.
The play of light and air rings magic changes,
Which strongly penetrate the soul anew
Even today, after three-thousand years;
And from the memory-pictures in the elements . . .

This places Tintagel's origin as a mystery centre just at the time mentioned above, compatible with the Bronze Age carving in Rocky Valley (which Steiner was not shown). From his lectures a few days later[i] we find that he experienced this centre as active under the leadership of successive 'Arthurs' almost up to the historical figure sought by historians and archaeologists. (Triad 56 indeed records three different fathers for the persons of Gwenhwyvar, his queens, a fact not yet explained on any other basis.)

In the Torquay lecture he said: 'There one can perceive a wonderful interplay between the light and the air, but also between the elemental spirits living in light and air. One can see spirit-beings streaming to the earth in the rays of the sun, one can see them mirrored in the glittering raindrops, one can see that which comes under the sway of earthly gravity appearing in the air as the denser spirit-beings of the air. Again, when the rain ceases and the rays of the sun stream through the clear air, one perceives the elemental spirits intermingling in a different way. There one witnesses how the sun works in earthly substance . . . In the days of King Arthur, special conditions were required in order that the spirituality so wondrously revealed and borne in by the sea might flow into their mission and their tasks. But to take hold of the spirit-forces working there in nature would have been beyond the power of one individual alone. A group of men was necessary, one of whom felt himself as the representative of the sun in the centre, and whose twelve companions were trained in such a way that in temperament, disposition and manner of acting, all of them together formed a twelvefold whole—such was the Round Table.'

We may gain some idea of the men concerned, from Greek reports of a certain Abaris, said to have come from Hyperborea—whether Tintagel or an Irish mystery centre is immaterial—around 530 BC, and to have instructed Pythagoras (580-500 BC) in philosophy. His name meant in Cornish 'representative of corn', hence he was probably a priest of Ceridwen. According to Himerius (AD 315-386) he came with a bow in his hand and a quiver (probably containing a sheaf of corn) on his shoulder. 'He was easy in address, agreeable in conversation, active in despatch, and secret in the management of great affairs; quick in judging present events, and ready to take part in any emergency . . . trusted with everything for his prudence. He spoke Greek with such fluency that you would have thought that he had been bred or brought up in the Lyceum, and had conversed all his life with the Academy of Athens.' His writings dealt with medicine, plague and epidemics.

We gain another glimpse from Cyprian of Antioch (AD 200-258), who described his forty-day initiation at Tempe, a temple of Apollo on the banks of the Pinios in Thessaly, to which Hyperboreans still came regularly. He was taught there the meaning of musical sounds, and the causes of growth and decay in herbs, trees and bodies; he had visions of tree trunks and magical herbs, and of the succession of the seasons; and he watched dramatic performances of *daimones* chanting, warring, deceiving and confounding each other.[25] Herodotus (485-425 BC) states that the rites of Delos also originated in Hyperborea.

The 'true Celts' arrived in waves between the seventh and first centuries BC, a period roughly corresponding to the Iron Age. Their chief god was Belinus ('ram'), Welsh Beli; and this was the age of Aries (Ram) beginning in 747 BC. There can be no doubt that the worship of Beli replaced that of Bran over most of Britain—Graves has established this[12] in connection with the poem 'The Battle of the Trees', and it is confirmed in the tale of 'Branwen' in the *Mabinogion*, and by Geoffrey of Monmouth in the battle between Brennius and his brother Belinus (who adds that they were later reconciled against the common enemy of Rome). This was probably about 400 BC.

But more inscriptions, more widely distributed including Rome itself, are devoted to Epona, the horse goddess. Although the horse existed in Britain from the earliest times, the Celts owed much of their success to the fact that they were fine horsemen, and made the horse their cult-animal. Many reminders of this, including very rich trappings, have been found and it is confirmed in the many 'Triads of the Horses'. In the horse the cosmic forces are drawn down into the head, as one can see from its very fine form, and it has long been rightly considered a symbol of intelligence, which began to develop in this age. Graves made a good case that the Bardic alphabet was introduced by the priests of Beli (those of Bran avoiding writing except for the secular use of Greek); and the abstract signs of writing marked the beginnings of intellectuality.

It is noteworthy that Glastonbury, the seat of Arthur's opponent Mordred/Melwas, who abducted Gwenhwyvar, was known as the island of Avallach son of Beli, whilst Arthur was associated with Bran. Many Welsh genealogies lead back to the 'marriage' of Beli with Don, the Welsh form of Danu/Anu, which implies the merging of the new religion with the ancient religion of Ireland, held among Irish settlers in north-west Wales. The complex story of the house of Don is told in the *Mabinogion* under the title of 'Math son of Mathonwy'.

But from the moment when Christ descended to earth, everything was changed. The atmosphere itself was now swathed in the living forces of Christ which had previously lived in the sunlight streaming to earth. There were a few men to whom this change was actually perceptible—the knights of the Round Table (Chapter 4.1). But it was still through their connection with these forces of Christ that they spread their culture, purifying the still wild and uncivilized soul forces, depicted in the legends as giants and monsters, of the then barbarous population of northern and central Europe.

5. An Inworld Journey

Against this broad background, we now turn to the extant documents, and consider as our first key to the mysteries of Arthur an early poem, *Preiddeu Annwn*, thought to date from about the tenth century. The text is severely corrupt, and emendations and interpretations by different scholars have varied unusually widely. The version which follows is based on the most recent study by M. Haycock,[20] but with some variants (for reasons mentioned in the Preface) from the options in her footnotes and from earlier specialists.

The poem describes an expedition across the 'water' to a series of island fortresses in the realm of Annwn, literally the 'in-world'. This world was conceived in Goidelic Dyved as populated not by the dead, but by creative and beautiful immortal beings, and was not always visible, but lit up and vanished suddenly. Its ruler was Arawn (eloquence) i.e., it was the kingdom of the divine Word. We shall see that the journey pictures the path of the soul from birth, through death and out through the cosmos, in preparation for the ensuing lifetime. The journey is made in Arthur's ship Prydwen ('white aspect', the purified soul), and at each step there is a refrain referring to a sevenfold return. This may hint at the seven stages of the soul world itself (Chapter 4.1) through which Arthur has to 'come back up' from yet deeper spiritual levels of consciousness. We saw that the tale of 'Branwen' described an expedition to Ireland (often representing the otherworld in Welsh legend) and named seven who returned, including Pryderi ('deep thought') son of Pwyll, Head of Annwn, and also Taliesin, purported author of this poem.

The first verse starts with birth into the physical world, the descent of Gweir (the infant name of Pryderi) from 'the extent of the world' into the prison of the body:

> I praise the lord, the sovereign of the royal realm
> Who has extended his sway over the extent of the world.
> The prison of Gweir was prepared in Fort Sidi (the otherworld)
> In the tale about Pwyll and Pryderi.
> No one before him went into it—
> Into the heavy blue chain restraining the loyal youth,
> And because of the spoils from the inworld he was singing bitterly,
> And our poetic invocation shall last until judgement day.
> Thrice the fullness of Prydwen we went into it;
> Save seven, none came back up from Fort Sidi.

The lord of the soul is the ego, and the sovereign of its realm is the higher ego that entends beyond a single life and passes from one incarnation to another through the whole extent of the world. Gweir's prison was the castle of Oeth and Anoeth (Triad 61) which was comprised of bones, i.e., the physical body. This is indeed prepared in the otherworld (Fort Sidi, Irish 'síde'); and its venous blood holds the blue chain of individual destiny that ties one down to the coming incarnation. But the soul will always long for the 'spoils' experienced in the supersensible world before birth, and will seek to regain them. We seem to be led to the very first incarnation, the expulsion from paradise, and the continuation until the Last Judgement; but 'judgement day' may refer rather to the judgement of the individual soul at death (pictured by Michael with the scales).

The next verse concerns experience after death, the four turrets of a fort representing the four phases of the moon (see Chapters 3.2 to 3.5). The 'I am' rises out of the body and receives its first inspiration from the dark blue bowl of heaven with its star-pearls:

> 'I am', renowned of fame: the song was heard
> In the four-turreted fort, perfectly revolving.
> My first utterance was spoken concerning the cauldron;
> By the breath of nine maidens this was kindled.
> The cauldron of the inworld's chief, what is its power?
> Dark blue, and pearls around its rim,
> It will not boil the food of a coward, it has not been so destined.
> The flashing sword of destruction was raised to it,
> And in the hand of the leaping one it was left;
> And before the threshold of the cold place, a lantern was burning.
> And when we went with Arthur—glorious hardship—
> Save seven, none came back up from Fort Veddwit (mead-feast).

The nine maidens are exemplified in another poem ascribed to Taliesin:[21] 'There are nine ranks of the mystic troops of heaven; and the tenth, that of the saints, prepares for the seventh age.' Their names in Christian tradition are known from Dionysius the Areopagite and comprise the divine

Hierarchies serving the Trinity. Pomponius Mela (c. AD 45) reported that there were in Britain 'nine priestesses, of great genius and rare endowments, capable of raising storms by their incantations, of transforming into what animals they please, curing ailments reckoned by others to be beyond the reach of medicine, quick at discerning and able to foretell what is to come, easy of address only to seafarers and those who come on purpose to consult them.' Arthur and his companions are such 'seafarers' in this poem.

The final verses make clear that 'cowards' were those who would not tread the path of spiritual development, and the cauldron 'will not boil the food of a coward' because only the spiritual striving of the individual is of service to these Hierarchies, whose work is the further evolution of mankind. The sword of thinking, which at the intellectual stage creates the weapons of destruction we see around us, can however be burnished (Chapter 3.6) and raised to this sphere, remaining fully under control in the hands of one who leaps for the heights. The 'lantern' which then shines into the inworld is clearly shown on the 'Moses' by Michelangelo and in paintings by Botticelli and others; the name Taliesin indeed means such a 'radiant brow'; and a later chapter will identify this as the supersensible organ known as the two-petal lotus flower. The realm of the 'mead-feast' pictures the sphere of social relationships, where the effects of one's deeds on other people become conscious—in eastern terminology the realm of kamaloca (Chapter 3.5).

The third verse takes us further, to the whole sphere traversed by the sun as experienced from the earth, of which the visible sun is the 'radiant door':

'I am', splendid in fame: the song is heard
In the quartered fort, the island of the radiant door.
Noonday and jet black are mingled.
Sparkling was the drink set before their host.
Thrice the fullness of Prydwen we went on the ocean,
Save seven, none came back up from Fort Rigor (firmness, vigour).

The image of the sun in man is the human heart, which reveals its quartered nature, albeit differently from the moon. In the sun, the very source of light, the separation between light and dark is transcended. The sun is the door from the soul world to spiritland (Chapter 4.1), where all is of an inner light. The initiate here drinks the sparkling nectar of the sun-beings—the Exusiai, Spirits of Form or 'firmness'; the Dynamis, Spirits of Movement or 'vigour'; and the Kyriotetes, Spirits of Wisdom—in their 'royal assembly' (an alternative reading of 'Fort Rigor').

The next verse takes us to the realm of the fixed stars:

> I do not deal with readers of the Lord's literature
> Who had not seen Arthur's valour beyond the glass/radiant fort.
> Three score hundred men stood on its wall,
> It was difficult to converse with their watchmen.
> Thrice the fullness of Prydwen went with Arthur;
> Save seven, none came back up from Fort Golud
>   (frustration, impediment).

The furthest stage of the adventure is one of valour, not of scholarship. The six thousand men on the wall probably represent the stars of the Milky Way; and communion with them would understandably be the most frustratingly difficult of all. (Incidentally this verse is reported by Nennius[22] as an event of the year 826, when Merfyn the Freckled, a man of exceptional calibre, gained power in Gwynedd; and it may be due to him that old epics such as this were first written down.)

The fifth verse brings us back to the zodiac, and specifically to Taurus:

> I do not deal with insignificant men with slack girdles,
> Who know not on what day mankind is created
> Nor in what hour of the day God was born,
> Nor who made those who did not go to the meadows of God (?)
> They know not of the speckled ox, with its stout collar
> And seven-score links in its fastening.
> When we went with Arthur, an awkward expedition,
> Save seven, none came back up from Fort Vandwy
>   (high God?).

This points to the preparation of the star-body or astral body for the coming incarnation, the 'day mankind is created', and to when the new ego, the god within it, is born. In the Taurean age (that of Hu and his oxen), when the Arthurian mysteries were founded, it would be natural to seek a special impulse from 'the speckled ox', with the zodiac as its 'collar' with sevenfold planetary fastening.

> I do not deal with readers of feeble intent,
> Who do not know on what day the lord was created,
> Nor at what time the ruler was born,
> Nor what animal they keep, silver its head.
> When we went with Arthur, a woeful encounter,
> Save seven, none came back up from Fort Ochren
>   (source of life).

Despite the similarity to the last verse, this brings us back to the moon sphere (silver is the moon metal). Here the unresolved impulses from the previous incarnation ('the animal they keep') are incorporated into the life-body, or etheric body, the 'source of life', for the new incarnation.

The seventh verse brings us down to the elements of fire, air and water:

> The monks throng together like a wolf pack
> Because of the encounter with the masters who know
> Whether every wind holds to one course, whether sea is a
> single water,
> Whether fire—invincible tumult—is from a single spark.

We are now back in the cloister, there is no cause to refer to Arthur and 'coming back up'. The contrast is drawn between the monks who still live as a group guided by a group-soul of the monastery, and the individuality of the masters who are conscious in the supersensible world and know the unity of things: the student of scripture, and the one who researches the wholeness of the divine forces at work throughout the cosmos.

The monks throng together like wolves
Because of the encounter with the masters who know.*
They do not know when darkness divides from dawn,
Or the course of the wind, what is its onrush,
What place it devastates, what land it strikes,
How many saints in the void, and how many in the world.
I praise the lord, the great sovereign.
May I not be sad: Christ be my reward.

The monks cannot distinguish the moment of dawn because they remain indoors, and do not connect sunrise with Christ as a Sun-Being—it was in 'one hour of dawn' that Myrddin experienced the 'seven-score and seven apple trees' (Chapter 5.3). Nor do they know the course of the wind, here signifying spirit (the words 'pneuma' in Greek and 'ruach' in Hebrew each mean both 'wind' and 'spirit'), because the concept of spirit as distinct from soul had been anathematized by the 8th Ecumenical Council of the Roman Church in 869. Note that the saints are characterized as living 'in the void', i.e., in the non-spatial cosmos. The poet however praises the individual ego, as lord and sovereign of the soul, i.e., as spirit; and he therefore feels confident of inheriting the kingdom of Christ, a kingdom of spirit bringing to mankind the precious impulse of individuality that was first nourished in the Celtic church and later rose again at the Reformation.

6. Nennius

The earliest reference of any length to Arthur, which has become the starting point of innumerable studies and must be our second key, is usually ascribed to Nennius, a monk at Bangor in North Wales, who about 830 AD compiled a Latin

---

* An alternative interpretation[22] of the second line of these last two verses: 'Because of the encounter of the lord with the swine-sorceress' is tempting, although less probable; for we shall find cumulative evidence that the Arthurian mysteries were represented by the symbol of the pig. Cuchulain was initiated by a 'sorceress', Scathach; and in the story of Taliesin (Chapter 5.4) Ceridwen is described as a sorceress.

History of the Britons[22] from source-material in Welsh. His main reference to Arthur is the famous list of twelve battles; but let us first get the measure of the author by means of three other relevant extracts. Two are in an appendix, and relate to the area between Hereford and Brecon where he may have been brought up. The first describes a mound in which is buried Amir, son of Arthur, of which he says that 'Arthur himself killed him and buried him there. And when men come to measure the length of the mound they find it sometimes 6ft, sometimes 9, sometimes 12, and sometimes 15ft. Whatever length you find it at one time, you will find it different at another, and I myself have proved this to be true.' Nennius is clearly not writing factually, but conveying some personal experience in veiled language, which is significant for him. What this may be we shall have to consider in a later section.

His second marvel describes a heap of stones at Builth, on top of which is one bearing the footprint of Arthur's dog Cabal. 'And men will come and carry away that stone for a day and a night, and next morning it will be back on its heap.' Again the original meaning is veiled—a cairn marking the rise of the dog-star (Sirius) from some menhir, perhaps?

Thirdly, Nennius sets against the year 826 the report (referred to in the last section) of a raid by ship on an island fortress of glass, whose watchmen are supernatural beings and do not reply to a challenge.

The material transcribed here is clearly not physical fact, as Nennius must have well known. When therefore we find Henry of Huntingdon saying in 1170 that the places named in the battle-list 'cannot be found', we may take him literally as meaning that he knew that they, too, were not historical. Modern scholars have made strenuous efforts to identify the places, but have not reached agreement compatible with the known historical situation. What then does the list describe?

T. Jones has pointed out[23] that the names of the battles suggest the rhyme-scheme of 'a Welsh poem of quite other provenance'—Dubglas/Bassas, Celidon/Guinnion, Legion/Bregion. He also remarks that the original Welsh expression translated into Latin as '*dux bellorum*' is likely to have been one which meant 'leader of a host', but not necessarily 'leader of battles'. Instead of trying to find the names on the map, let us therefore consider the text incorporating the translations of these names from the Welsh, so far as Kenneth Jackson was able to give them.[24]

The excerpt starts with an illuminated capital, indicating a fresh source, and begins: 'Arthur fought against them alongside the kings of Britain, but he himself was leader of a host.' Some versions add: 'there were many more noble than he.' Although the previous Latin sentence concerned the Saxons, the fact that a new source is being collated means that it is not clear to what the word 'them' refers. It will be noted that there is no implication that Arthur was a king—indeed neither he nor Gwenhwyvar figure in any early genealogical list; it is only much later that he begins to be claimed as ancestor for reasons of political prestige. But neither was he subservient to the kings, for he led a host—the task of a king—and fought alongside them. This suggests that he had similar authority, such as that of a spiritual leader. It had been normal practice for a chief druid to give the king spiritual support in battle, much as the church today offers prayers for queen and country; hence, for him to fight 'alongside' the kings as spiritual leader would be nothing new. It is noteworthy that Gildas the historian, probably writing before the battle of Camblan, does not mention Arthur, perhaps knowing that he was not a temporal leader.

The text continues: 'The first battle was in the mouth of the river called "pure, gleaming" (Glein). The second, third, fourth and fifth were on another river which is called "black-blue" (Dubglas) and is in the region of Linnuis/Inniis. The sixth was upon a river called "shallow" (Bassas). The seventh was in the wood of Celidon, that is "the battle of Celidon wood" (this phrase a repetition in Welsh). The eighth was in "white castle" (Guinnion), in which Arthur carried on his shoulders an image of St Mary Ever-Virgin, and there was great slaughter of them through the strength of Our Lord Jesus Christ and of the holy Mary His maiden-mother. The ninth battle was in the city of the Legions. The tenth was on the river-shore called "variegated in colour or surface" (Tribruit). The eleventh was on the hill called Agned (meaning unknown) or Bregion (hills). The twelfth was on mount Badon, in which on that one day there fell in one onslaught of Arthur nine-hundred and sixty men; and none slew them but he alone, and in all his battles he remained victor.' This last remark should again serve to confirm that this document is not concerned with reporting historical fact!

We may at this point recall from Chapter 2.1 how Rudolf Steiner spoke at Tintagel about 'the experience of the knights of Arthur, who experienced in this eternal struggle of the forces of light with the elements of the earth a reflection of their own inner battles, where in the realm of soul and spirit, light and darkness battle for mastery, and the ego force, the illuminated consciousness of man, strives to achieve in ceaseless battle mastery over the clouds and fog of the passions.' This draws attention to a different class of battles, the reality of which everyone can, by appropriate effort, verify personally.

Such a consideration must lead to the question whether the battle-list is a more detailed sketch of the expedition described in *Preiddeu Annwn*. Looking at it in this light, we find that the names are nearly all descriptive, and that three of them stand out from the remainder which are merely listed. The grouping of four battles together 'on the river black-blue' recalls the 'four-pointed fort perfectly revolving'; and any artist painting a moonlit scene would work in indigo. In contrast 'white castle' immediately suggests bright sunlight, and mention of Christ and His mother at this point brings in a new quality of spirituality. Thirdly, Arthur's marvellous feats at the last battle called 'highlands' look as though they might correspond to his valour 'beyond the glass fort', of which we saw that Nennius was aware. We find further that the number of intermediate battles corresponds to the number of intermediate planets.

We therefore suggest as a working hypothesis that the battle list gives a sequence of inner battles on the path of initiation into the mysteries of the cosmos which were being carried forwards from megalithic times. Such an initiation, which requires strong moral development, could well have been a prerequisite for kingship in pre-Christian times, as it was for the Pharaohs. In that case Arthur, in the role of hierophant, literally fought these battles 'alongside' the kings. It is suggested that Nennius was transmitting, perhaps unknowingly, a note concerning these mysteries, to the guarded extent that it had been thought prudent to put this in writing before the ninth century. It is further suggested that up to the twelfth century, certain parts of this substance were elaborated, in order to preserve them, in the form of legends, which may be coordinated by the battle list.

In the next two chapters this hypothesis will be tested, with particular reference to a third key, the great tale of *Culhwch and Olwen* in the *Mabinogion*. This is thought to have been composed in the tenth century—a century earlier than any of the romances—from material of which parts may reach back to pre-Christian times, although the earliest manuscript only dates from 1325. Other Welsh material will be adduced in support, consideration of the Chronicles and continental Romances being, in the main, deferred until a later chapter, for reasons which will become apparent.

We may thus be able to gain entry in some detail into the successive inner battles of the soul, as it trod at least the earlier stages of the path of development in the Arthurian mysteries.

CHAPTER THREE

BATTLES OF THE SOUL

1. The Gleaming Estuary

The first verse of *Preiddeu Annwn* dealt with the descent of Gweir from the realm of Caer Sidi, where his body had been made ready, to physical incarnation. One can well picture the soul's existence before birth as a 'pure, gleaming stream' of spiritual experiences, and birth as the mouth of this river as it enters the ocean of earthly life.

Before the thirteenth century, and especially before the fourth, traces of atavistic clairvoyance were common—the sketches of man in Fig. 1 still depict the aura—and the gate of birth was still open, so that vision into the life before birth in the supersensible world was still possible. Indeed, even in the nineteenth century William Wordsworth could still write:

> Our birth is but a sleep and a forgetting:
> The Soul that rises with us, our life's Star,
> Hath had elsewhere its setting,
> And cometh from afar:
> Not in entire forgetfulness,
> And not in utter nakedness,
> But trailing clouds of glory do we come
> From God, who is our home.

There are many accounts of marvellous births and precocious childhoods, not only in Arthurian literature but also in Irish sources, the Welsh *Mabinogion* (a word which itself once meant 'tales of youth') and in many lives of the saints. After summarizing the features of over thirty such births in Celtic literature, A. and B. Rees conclude:[1] 'The child is the incarnation of a supernatural essence; animal correlatives emphasize the extra-human, otherworldly, unconscious side of the hero's nature... He is usually an embarrassment to someone, and the attempt is made to get rid of him... Resistance is a constant feature—disturbances from the otherworld must be repressed.'

A good example is Geoffrey of Monmouth's description [2] of the birth of the Merlin who prophesied before Vortigern. His mother was said to have been visited many times in her private apartments with her sister nuns by a spirit 'of a nature that doth partake both of men and angels' in the form of a most handsome young man, who then vanished, or sometimes spoke without becoming visible. This being made love to her and made her pregnant. Geoffrey quotes Apuleus as authority for the authenticity of such an event, but we might support him from Genesis 6 i-iv: 'the sons of God came in unto the daughters of men, and they bare children to them: the same were the mighty men which were of old, the men of renown.'

Steiner spoke of such a phenomenon[3] as characteristic of an initiate in the North (to whom such legends refer). The body provided by the parents does not conform with his unusual individuality, his inner driving force conflicts with the surrounding world, and he therefore feels dissatisfied with his destiny. People have no insight or feeling to help them understand him, perhaps only one of them has any inkling of what is developing in him, and they feel an instinctive hatred of him. The child is truly 'amid wild beasts' both inwardly and outwardly. Such an individuality may be indwelt by a higher being without having risen to lofty heights himself, in order to become a leader of men and to come to know the Beings of the spiritual world. Such conflicts are inevitable if there is to be real progress.

Pre-natal life is described most fully in the *Hanes Taliesin*[4] in the story of little Gwion, who at birth became Taliesin. Gwion was 'in the beginning of Arthur's time' charged to kindle the fire beneath the cauldron of Ceridwen. This cauldron was filled with charm-bearing herbs that had been gathered daily 'according to the books of the astronomers and in planetary hours.' Towards the end of a year it chanced that three drops of 'the grace of Inspiration' splashed onto Gwion's finger, and, putting it to his mouth because of the great heat (as did his namesake Fionn in Ireland and Sigurd in Scandinavia), he 'foresaw everything that was to come'; the cauldron thereupon burst, shedding its contents as poison. Ceridwen's cauldron represents, in the imaginative language of the time, the bowl of the sky. From it is born the human astral (starry) body, which has three aspects—thinking, feeling and willing. Everything that is to come in the new incarnation is foreseen—we are reminded of the effect of Eve's eating the forbidden apple in the Garden of Eden, the knowledge of good and evil, and the expulsion from Paradise. When the contents of the cauldron spill onto the earth as the foundation of consciousness, they work in opposition to the life-processes, and hence resemble a poison—were it not for this, growth would go on and on and on. Taliesin later says of this: 'In the hall of Ceridwen was I first modelled in the form of a pure man . . . I was great . . . My destiny was imparted to me without audible language by the old giantess, darkly smiling in her wrath...'

When Ceridwen discovers what has happened, she chases Gwion and he flees. He changes into a hare and she into a greyhound; he into a fish and she into an otter; he into a bird and she into a hawk; he into a grain of wheat in a barn, and she into a black hen who swallows him. Here we have represented the elements of earth, water, air and heat respectively. On the last step towards incarnation we draw together in the moon sphere these elements forming the etheric body. When, after nine months, she is delivered of Gwion in human form, Ceridwen could not in her heart do him harm, so 'she wrapped him in a leather bag, and cast him into the sea at the

mercy of God'. He is born, like Moses, into the ocean of earthly
space. Caught in a weir, the scaffolding of the hereditary
physical body, he is then found on Mayday and called Taliesin.

Looking now at *Culhwch*, we find that the story starts with
a marvel-birth: Culhwch's mother, called 'Bright Day', an aunt
of Arthur, 'got a son through the prayers of the country', or
was connected in a special way with the inspiring Folk Spirit.
'But from the time she grew with child she went mad, without
coming near a dwelling'—she was peculiarly open to cosmic
influences. 'When her time came upon her, her right sense
came back to her in a place where a swineherd was keeping
a herd of swine, and through terror of the swine the queen
was delivered. And the swineherd took the boy until he came
to court.' We shall find cumulative evidence in what follows
that the Arthurian mysteries were represented by the image
of the pig, and may conclude that the boy was fostered in such
a mystery place under the direction of the 'swineherd'. The
boy was even named Culhwch, explained to mean 'pig-run',
and his tale reaches its climax in a boar-hunt. But the queen,
Bright Day, the gleaming river, dies—prenatal experience of
the spiritual sun-forces is lost. The king promised not to
remarry until he saw a two-headed briar on her grave, which
happened after seven years, the time when a child's own
etheric body is fully independent.[5]

The lad is subsequently brought to court by his stepmother,
presumably at puberty. When he declines her daughter, she
swears on him the destiny to marry Olwen, daughter of the
Chief Giant. 'The boy coloured, and love of the maiden entered
into every limb of him, although he had never seen her.' It
is at this age that the astral (soul) forces bearing the destiny
become fully active,[5] and the stepmother is therefore able to
express 'what is to come'. Whereas on the descent to incarnation the starry body is formed before the etheric, after physical
birth the etheric body comes to fruition before the astral.

Whilst both Peredur and Tristan are characterized as youths
of exceptional abilities, there is nothing marvellous in the story
of the birth or upbringing of either. But Parzival weeps at the

beauty of bird song because it reminds him of pre-earthly joys he has lost. Geoffrey of Monmouth's well-known story of the birth of Arthur himself through the magic of Merlin will be considered at a later stage (Chapter 7.1).

The mysteries of incarnation and birth, of how the body was formed and how it had evolved to its present condition, were known in ancient time as the Mysteries of the Father, the highest of all mysteries. Gradually the ability to look back through this Gate of Birth came to an end. Nevertheless, the first battle of the soul was at that time to keep it as open as possible through a kind of spirit-recollection, so that this pure, gleaming stream might still bear some of its treasures into the ocean of life.

* * * * *

There follows in *Culhwch* a lyrical description, magnificently perceived in its physical detail, of the lad setting out with his horse, dogs and accoutrements of spiritual power to get Arthur's help to find and achieve Olwen. He arrives to find the gate of Arthur's court shut for the night; but the gatekeeper Glewlwyd is persuaded by the threat of three shouts that would make every woman at court barren to consult Arthur—i.e., Culhwch not only threatens to close the Gate of Birth, but also threatens the land's fertility, and thus Arthur's very sovereignty. Glewlwyd confides to Arthur that in all their travels together he has never seen the like of Culhwch (candidates for the mysteries were selected by perception of their aura). Arthur admits him, and 'what every man did, to dismount on the horse-block at the gate, he did not do; but on his steed he came inside', and greeted equally all in the hall: he takes his intelligence—represented by the horse—into Arthur's realm, and practises real democracy. Twice tempted by offers of food and entertainment, he pursues his objective of seeking help from Arthur, who warms to his importunity despite the remonstrance of Cei. He requests and receives a hair trim at Arthur's hand, a symbol of acceptance into the community, and discloses his kinship.

Next comes an extraordinary list of 240 people in whose name Culhwch invokes the boon of Arthur's help. It includes the only three survivors of the battle of Camblan in which Arthur was mortally wounded, thus suggesting that his court is in the otherworld. The list also includes most of the names known to early Welsh tradition, many otherwise unknown, marvel-workers, comic characters, relatives of Arthur, and ladies of the court. It appears chaotic in translation; the original text, however, forms rhythmic units which contain alliteration, rhyme (both assonance and consonance) and groups of cognate words. Who could have known all these characters and have expressed them in such a poetic way? We are being delicately told that Culhwch had as a youth already reached the level of a bard—his foster-father, probably the 'swineherd', had indeed given him a training in the lesser mysteries. The whole scene may thus be taken as a characterization of the stage of Probation. But this is not sufficient to find Olwen: for a year Arthur's messengers search for her in vain.

2. The Plain of Death

The Twilight of the Gods, the closing of the gate of birth into the supersensible world, was deeply experienced not only in the Northern mysteries—to which it gave a specially tragic tone—but also in others. The only alternative way out of the limitations of the sense-world was the so-called gate of death: how could the pupil of the mysteries pass through this gate without actually succumbing to death? That was the question to which all mysteries had to find an answer.

In *Culhwch* we find that before the enterprise begins, Arthur assembles a small group to accompany Culhwch. This consists of three knights, Cei (pronounced 'Kye'), Gwalchmei and Bedwyr; and three 'wonder-workers', Cynddylig the Guide, Gwrhyr Interpreter of Tongues, and Menw the Enchanter. We shall need to assess the symbolism of the three knights, Arthur's constant companions, when all the material is to hand (Chapter

8.3); but we are already given here a lot of information about Cei, who takes the initiative. For example, a wound from his sword no physician might heal; whatever burden he carries will never be seen; what he holds will be kept dry by his great heat, enough to kindle a fire; yet he will have no heat in his hands, and his heart will be cold. This can only be reconciled by regarding him as a personification of thinking, the two-edged sword which may be intellectualistic or creative. The ever-courteous Gwalchmei, Arthur's nephew, never returns without the quest he seeks, and stands for the constant nobility of the feeling life. The handsome Bedwyr, of whom we rarely hear much—no three warriors drew blood faster than he— seems to represent the strong silent will that works unconsciously, directly into the blood.

Menw (Little, son of Three Shouts, i.e., of the threefold Word) is otherwise known from a bardic text of questioned authenticity.[6] This tells how he saw shining from the mouth of Einigen (Enoch) in his grave three rays of light, which the latter had received from God, and which comprised the whole of knowledge and science. From these rays was formed the symbol /|\, which was the basis of the bardic alphabet (similar to Ogham). Nothing further is known of Cynddylig or Gwrhyr, but the three together seem to hint at the wonders that a child unfolds during his first three years and that distinguish man from the animals: upright walking (the guide), speaking (the interpreter of tongues), and the capacity to think (Menw). Thus a party of seven is formed, including Culhwch. In other words, the candidate must 'pull together' the forces of soul and spirit within his inner life.

Now the quest begins in earnest. The party come to a wide open plain, and see ahead 'the greatest of forts in the world. That day they journeyed. When they thought they were near to the fort, they were no nearer than at first. And the second and the third day they journeyed, and with difficulty did they get thereto.' (Three days was the typical period of initiation in the mysteries.) They encounter a shepherd with a huge mastiff, and 'no company had ever fared past him that he did not do it harm or deadly hurt; every dead tree and bush that was on the plain, his breath would burn them to the very ground.' The shepherd stands at the Threshold of Death, for we soon hear that all previous suitors and 23 of the shepherd's own sons have been killed by the giant whose fort he guards.

In *Owein or The Lady of the Fountain* (referred to subsequently simply as *Owein*) the adventure starts in 'the bounds of the world and its wilderness' before descending into a forest. In *Peredur* the lad travels desert and wilderness and then a great forest. Other legends start in the darkness of a forest, often in search of some magical beast. The *Elucidation* prefixed to Chrestien's *Perceval* explains why the land was dead, a desert: a wicked king had violated one of the maidens who had nourished travellers with whatever food they wished; and he had carried off her gold cup, and caused himself to be served out of it. 'The realm then turned to waste, never did a tree have a leaf, the meadows and flowers dried up, and the streams shrunk away.' It was Arthur's task to restore the land from the barren consequences of the egoism of the 'wicked king'.

The barren plain can here be recognized as an image of the loss of awareness of the spirit, and the consequent sensual desires for material things. 'The mind of the flesh is death', Paul wrote to the Romans. It is the situation of which John the Baptist said: 'I am the voice of one crying in the wilderness, "Make straight the path of the Lord".' After the abduction of Persephone by Hades, Demeter no longer fructified the land. Our civilization today lives in the grip of such material desires, its ideas mainly restricted to that which can be counted, measured or weighed. And this is an absolutely necessary stage in evolution. If we are to become independent spiritual beings, the leading-strings in our consciousness to the Beings who have created us must be cut, or else we should remain mere puppets. This is our starting point, and we must progress beyond it, but in the past it could only be reached by a conscious effort to exclude the all-pervasive remnants of spiritual traditions.

To progress, we must face the facts of death and loneliness, as if the ground had been taken from under our feet, and quieten the mastiff by deliberately laying aside in special moments all sense-experiences, both of the world and of our own body. We are sustained by the faculties of clear imaginative thinking and sound moral discernment, 'the burning lantern' (Chapter 2.5), the two-petal lotus flower* in the brow (Plate 5).

We may fairly describe this stage as a moonscape; thus we come to the second battle of Nennius, the first of the four on the river 'black-blue' (Dubglas). At this first stage, that of new moon, we are in darkness; only when we have laid aside our glowing desires for sensual satisfaction will the moonlight gradually begin to shine.

3. The Gatekeeper

Those who in all ages and cultures have reached the gate of death, know that the supersensible world is separated from the visible world by a distinct threshold of consciousness comparable to that between sleeping and waking. And their first experience at this threshold is the meeting with a purely spiritual Being within them called the Guardian of the Threshold, whose task it is to guard the individual against entering the otherworld consciously before he is mature and morally ripe enough to do so safely: otherwise his consciousness is darkened into that of sleep.

This confrontation, which forms the third 'battle', is described in most spiritual traditions, the best known picture being that at the beginning of the Apocalypse. In the midst of seven lamps stands one 'like unto' a Son of Man, whose head and hair were white like wool as white as snow, his eyes like a flame of fire, and his voice like the sounding of many waters; in his right hand he held seven stars, from his mouth came a two-edged sword, and his countenance was like the sun shining

---

* The term 'lotus flower' will be described more fully in Chapter 4.4.

in its strength. 'And when I saw him I fell at his feet as one dead.'

This figure appears in Arthurian literature in varied forms—sometimes indeed in two forms in one tale. In *Culhwch* he first appears as Arthur's gatekeeper when the lad seeks to *enter* Arthur's hall. His name, Glewlwyd Gavelvawr, means 'Ancient Bold One of the Mighty Dominion'—an apt description of his function. He is only active himself because it is a special occasion, midwinter, and he has four deputies. He has accompanied Arthur on all his travels, thus emphasizing his universal nature. It is on his judgement that Arthur admits the comely lad.

Glewlwyd also makes a brief appearance at the beginning of *Owein*, where his task is 'to make known to guests the ways and usages of the court', and also in *Gereint*. He was called by Iolo Goch, a fourteenth-century poet, 'the man who raised the cauldron from the fire in one hand, with the dead flesh of seven oxen in it.' Since the 'oxen of Hu' are the planets, this picture echoes that of the Apocalypse.

In a poem *Pa Gur,*[7] thought from its diction to be as old as the sixth-eighth century, and to be based on still earlier traditions, the meeting with Glewlwyd is more fully described:

Arthur:	Who is gatekeeper?
Glewlwyd:	Ancient Bold One of the Mighty Dominion. Who asks?
Arthur:	Arthur, with worthy Cei.
Glewlwyd:	What support do you have?
Arthur:	The best men in the world.
Glewlwyd:	Into my realm you shall not come, unless you disclose them.
Arthur:	I will disclose them, and you shall see them.

Arthur, as leader of the mystery, brings before the Guardian his pupil Cei, whom he describes as worthy, or properly prepared. We saw earlier that the initiation process required the support of twelve helpers, and these are now named. They include three Irish gods of the Tuatha de Danaan: Manawydan, cognate with Manannan son of the Sea and lord of land-under-wave, the land of eternal youth or the inworld; Anwas the Winged, probably Aengus, who fell in love with an elf-king's daughter and flew off with her in the form of two swans; and Llwch Leminawc, Lugh of the many skills, the god of light. The presence of these gods in his retinue points to the fact that each 'Arthur' had to master the Hibernian mysteries or, as Geoffrey of Monmouth put it, to 'conquer Ireland'. (Compare Steiner's description in Chapter 2.4 of how the Knights at Tintagel experienced the interplay of the elemental beings in the sunlight with those rising from below in water and air.) Also included in the twelve are Mabon son of Modron (whom we meet in Chapter 3.6), Uther Pendragon's man (Ranulf?) and 'my nephew', namely Gwalchmei. The remaining three names are otherwise unknown and untranslated, and 'three sages' are mentioned. 'Outstanding would be my men in defence of their customs' says Arthur. The continuation of this poem will be considered later.

But in *Culhwch* the Guardian figure encountered at the beginning of the quest proper, as the party go *out* in search of Olwen, takes the form of the shepherd who with his mastiff guards the castle of the giant. His full name, Custennin, son of Exile, suggests that he exists through the exile of the soul from its spiritual home. After Menw has rendered the mastiff harmless, they greet Custennin with words recently translated[4] as 'How magnificent you are'—a greeting appropriate to a Being of the spiritual world. Custennin first tests them by trying to persuade them to turn back. Culhwch however gives him a gold ring, often representing the earthly ego and its knowledge of the sense world. It does not fit Custennin, so he takes it in his glove to his wife, who says pointedly 'the sea does not tolerate a dead man's jewel' (the soul world does not accept the jewel of the sense-world). She turns out to be an aunt of Culhwch, and her embrace as they approach her threshold would have proved fatal to Cei, had he not had the presence of mind to thrust into her hands a stake to squeeze instead—this pictures the danger of entering the soul world insufficiently prepared and alert. They enter, and their needs are supplied.

In *Owein* the Guardian is lightly sketched the second time as a man 'in his prime, with yellow curly hair and his beard new-trimmed, wearing a tunic and mantle of yellow brocade'—hence a sunlit figure—who was 'so courteous as to greet me before I could greet him, and he accompanied me into the fort.' In *Peredur* (Chapter 7.4) the Guardian is represented by the first uncle, a hoary-headed lame man sitting near a lake, who has a yellow-haired and an auburn-haired son. He tests Peredur, who has already defeated sixteen knights and sent them to Arthur's court, against the former. And it is he who teaches Peredur: 'though you see what is strange, do not ask about it. . . any rebuke will fall on me.' That is to say, he effectively prevents Peredur from making progress at that time.

The higher world cannot be properly entered without encountering this figure. All the flowing susceptibility of the soul has to be concentrated on the one and only reality: 'I am the door.'

4. Goreu and Olwen

After Culhwch's party have entered Custennin's house, his wife opens a chest by the hearth, and from it steps her twenty-fourth and lastborn son, a lad with curly yellow hair, who at the suggestion of Cei joins the party as an eighth member. He has no name at this point, but is later able to cross the three walls of Wrnach's castle (Chapter 3.6) 'as though it were nothing out of the way', and is then named Goreu, meaning 'best'. He takes part in the crucial struggle with the boar (Chapter 4.3). And it is he who finally cuts off the head of Giant Hawthorn and takes possession of all his dominions. Who is this mysterious figure?

Our only clue is in Triad 52, which relates that Arthur himself had been 'three nights in prison in Caer Oeth and Anoeth, and three nights imprisoned by Gwen Pendragon, and three nights in an enchanted prison under the stone of Echymeint. And it was the same lad who released him from

each of these prisons—Goreu, son of Custennin, his cousin.'
Now Caer Oeth and Anoeth (precious and wonderful) was said
to be constructed from human bones, and is thus the skeleton
of the physical body. Gwen (white) Pendragon may perhaps
be interpreted as consort of Uthyr Pendragon, namely the
earth-mother or life forces. And the stone of Echymeint
covered the cell of Ceridwen: it is the 'crystal heaven' above
the bowl of the stars from which the astral body is drawn
(Chapter 3.1). The release of Arthur from these three 'prisons'
thus points to his release from constraints of the threefold
body. As bringer of salvation to Arthur himself, Goreu, the best,
seems to stand for the one through whom the forces of
redemption come to mankind, namely Jesus. Goreu is revealed
from the 'chest' in the presence of Custennin as Guardian, but
only later exerts his full power.

At the corresponding point of the stories of *Perceval/Par-
zival* we find the Fisher King and the first appearance of the
Grail (Chapter 7.4), the vessel which bore the blood of Jesus;
but it is unattainable without much further effort.

* * * * *

Now that Culhwch has the support of Goreu, he is enabled
to have sight of Olwen, daughter of Chief Giant Hawthorn
(though she is never described as a giantess). She comes to
Custennin's house regularly to wash her hair, and 'always
leaves her rings in the bowl'. There is a charming description
of her which, apart from her yellow hair, is in terms of the
whiteness of her skin and the redness of her cheeks and robe—
the colours of otherworld beings in Welsh tradition. 'Even as
he saw her he knew her.' Whereas Culhwch's ring had been
rejected, hers—and she had many of them—are accepted. It
is she who brings the whole quest into action, standing
invisibly behind it until the very end, and she is thus an important figure. She seems to represent the eternal being that passes
through successive incarnations, leaving behind her successive
'rings'.

Culhwch at once expresses his love for her, his will to unite
with her. But she explains that when she marries, her father
the Chief Giant must die; and her marriage is not permitted
until all his demands have been met. Culhwch's quest for
Olwen was sworn on him as a matter of destiny; and the advice
Olwen gives him as the one and only means to obtain her—to
say 'yes' to every demand her father makes—means the acceptance of destiny, whether he likes it or not. All personal wishes
must here be set aside. And since destiny arises from all the
imperfections with which the individual has sullied the primal
nature given by the Father principle, to find out what is
demanded is at the same time the ancient demand of the
mysteries, and specifically of the mystery of Apollo: 'Know
yourself.'

We learn that four white trefoils spring up behind Olwen's
steps, thus a twelvefold pattern. Hence her name is interpreted
as 'white track'. But Homer called the trefoil the 'lotus';[9]
Olwen is connected with the organ known as the twelve-petal
lotus flower, which is located in the heart (Plate 6). She is
Culhwch's beloved, and he must first develop this spiritual
organ, which opens perception of the astral world to which
she belongs, to win her. And it is the presence of Goreu which
will enable him to do this.

In *Parzival*, Konduiramurs, and in *Peredur*, the beleaguered
maiden, are described in a way very similar to Olwen, except
that their hair is black. Parzival indeed marries the former at
once, but never meets her again until the Grail is achieved;
Peredur merely helps the latter, and she does not enter the
story again.

In *Owein* the figure 24 also appears, here in respect of the
maidens who (in four groups of six) look to the hero's needs.
They share in his meal with the man in yellow with curly hair,
as he tells Owein where to go and how to confront a huge black
man corresponding to the Chief Giant. The qualities of Goreu
and Olwen seem to be mixed together here. *Preiddeu Annwn*
does not identify this stage clearly, but reference in Verse 2
to the nine maidens who kindle the cauldron hints, as we saw,
at the breathing into man of divine forces.

The third of the moon stages (the fourth battle) is that of full moon, and we find a first reflection of the mysteries of the Sun and the possibility of redemption, but at this stage no more than a reflection: further trials must yet be endured.

5. Confronting the Giant(s)

Culhwch and his party now enter the fort of Ysbaddaden Chief Giant. 'Ysbaddaden' means Hawthorn, traditionally the tree of purification and chastity, from which the Crown of Thorns was made. This sets the tone for the fifth battle; the prose becomes dry and stark, like an Icelandic saga.

The encounter lasts three-and-a-half days, as so often in the Apocalypse and other legends. Thrice in succession the Giant hurls at them a poisoned spear of stone (he lives in a Stone-age consciousness); and each time the spear is caught and hurled back as a spear of iron. The first time Bedwyr pierces the ball of his knee, the second time Menw pierces the middle of his breast and the small of his back, and the third time Culhwch himself pierces one of his eyeballs and the nape of his neck. The Giant is thus mastered in the limbs, the rhythmic system and the head. Each time he curses the poisoned iron, the smith who fashioned it, or the forge where it was heated—he recognizes that it is the quality of iron, wrought magically by those who catch and at once return the spears, which is decisive for his undoing.

It is important to experience inwardly how the Giant is overcome by transforming, and *turning back* on him, his own spears. The three soul forces represented by the Giant, within the candidate for initiation, initially directed outwards towards the sense world, now have to be redirected inwards towards the soul itself. By doing so the thinking is strengthened through the effort of will involved in meditation; the will comes to be directed neither by impulse nor by dogmatic principle, but by thoughtful insight into the reality of the situation, that is to say, in freedom; and feeling is transformed from a purely personal reaction to a sensitivity for the soul-life of the world around which gives rise to it.[10] This whole inner battle—and it is a fierce one to win—involves the purging of that which is merely subjective, and enables Culhwch to take his seat beneath the Giant and undertake his every demand without qualm.

We are fortunate to possess another epic portrayal of this battle in the eighth-century Anglo-Saxon poem *Beowulf*,[11] although this comes from the Scandinavian rather than the Arthurian mysteries, and the three attacks are differentiated and reversed in sequence. Beowulf's first encounter is with a mighty fiend called Grendel, a notorious 'ranger of the borderlands', i.e., of the Threshold. Grendel, because of his disbelief, is incensed by a song that related the creation of man by God (do we not recognize how many offspring Grendel has today?). This contest takes place in the arched hall of the palace, representing the skull. No earthly blade could injure Grendel (doubt in God is not to be overcome by materialistic standards of thinking). So 'the resolute, cool-headed man' Beowulf wrestled with him, until he tore off the monster's arm and shoulder i.e., he mastered the will-impulses connected with the head) and Grendel fled mortally wounded to a lake of water-demons, where Beowulf later decapitated him. The second encounter took place 'deep under water' against Grendel's mother, who was 'impelled by intense hatred' and sought her revenge. With a special corselet to protect his breast, Beowulf followed her into the lake, which was filled with reptiles, dragons and serpents, and was carried off to her underground cavern. Here his own sword failed him, but with an ancient blade forged by giants which had been left hanging there, he slashed through her backbone, (i.e., he prevails not through his own capacity, but by grasping that which is available to him 'under the water'). Beowulf's third exploit was in old age, against a fire-breathing dragon guarding treasure in a cave by the sea shore. This struggle was 'to probe the resources of his soul, and tear the life from his body.' This 'winged worm' inspired such fear, that all Beowulf's kinsmen cowered behind trees; one alone helped him finally to rip open the belly of the worm, but in so doing a mortal poison bit deep into his own entrails.

Such brief reference to a great epic serves merely to outline its three aspects: head, breast and metabolic systems; disbelief, hatred and fear; consciousness within the hall, 'underwater', and within the cave of the earth.

Battles with three giants are not uncommonly described. For example we hear[12] that 'at a certain festivity of the Nativity of Caerleon the illuustrious king Arthur, having conferred military distinction upon a valiant youth of the name Ider, the son of king Nudd, in order to prove him, conducted him to the hill of Brent Noll for the purpose of fighting three most atrocious giants. And Ider, going before the rest of the company, attacked the giants valorously and slew them. And when Arthur came up he found him apparently dead, having fainted with the immense toil he had undergone; whereupon he reproached himself with having been the cause of his death through his tardiness in coming to his aid; and having arrived at Glastonbury, he appointed four and twenty monks to say mass for his soul, and endowed them most amply.'

In *Gereint* also there is brief reference to a battle with three giants, after which the hero 'falls from his horse as if dead'. Beowulf dies, Ider is 'apparently dead'. The fourth of the battles in the black-blue region of the moon leads back, as does the fourth moon quarter, to the new moon, the realm of darkness and death. But this death may now, as in the case of Ider, become a 'festival of nativity', birth into a higher realm.

In *Owein* this stage is only lightly sketched. The hero has to go back the way he came (the reversal of direction again), and then branch right until he reaches a huge black man seated on a mound, with only one foot and one eye, and a huge iron club. He is the 'keeper of the forest', to whom the wild animals 'as numerous as the stars in the firmament' do obeisance, i.e., he is master of the astral forces. He 'spoke nothing to me save incivility', yet in his rough manner tells the way forward.

This situation can be described from different points of view, the common factor being the purification of the candidate's inner life before stepping into a new realm where any remaining faults would be enhanced. Therefore careful preparation and rigorous tests were necessary to ensure that the moral forces had been sufficiently strengthened.

In *Preiddeu Annwn* (Chapter 2.5) the corresponding realm was summed up as 'fort Veddwit', translated as the 'mead feast'. This gives a very different impression, pointing to social relationships, hopefully congenial. And it is indeed at this stage after death that social relationships are experienced—but not, as here, from our own point of view, but from that of the other person.[13] If we caused someone pain in life, we now experience their pain; we realize that we owe it to them to compensate for it—this is indeed a joyful relief; and thus seeds are planted for our destiny together in a future life. But we need not wait until after death to do this, we can start right now, and it is a particular task of the candidate for initiation to bring order, not only into his inner life, but also into his human relationships. This is the 'mead-feast', where the cauldron will not boil the food of a coward. In eastern terminology it is the realm of 'kamaloca'.

* * * * *

We can now return to *Culhwch* and his party of seven. Chief Giant Hawthorn is required to name the marvels necessary to win his daughter, which he does in a repetitive formula reminiscent of an Indian sacred text. The first seven are concerned with the ploughing of ground so that meat and drink for the guests and flax for the wedding veil can be grown overnight. The next seven concern food, drink and entertainment for the wedding feast. Only the last task in these two groups is mentioned again, whereas all but one of those which follow are described or implied. These all, with the same exception, concern the shave and haircut of the Giant, the tools for the haircut having to be obtained from between the ears of the boar Twrch Trwyth. In one of them the Giant requires

Culhwch to obtain Arthur himself, whom he calls 'a man of mine', thereby raising the question of whom he sees himself to be.

These apparently random tasks do have a limited inherent logic. First we have emphasis on ploughing the earth, the physical foundation. Then the items for the feast point to stimulation of the life-processes of the etheric body. But these receive scant further attention. Fulfilment concentrates on the shave and haircut; and we may recall that when Samson's hair was cut he not only lost his strength, but 'the Lord departed from him' (Judges xvi): his link with the Father-forces was broken. Seven of the tasks refer specifically to the hunt: Drudwyn (Precious White), Garselit, Gwyn, Gwilenhin, son of Alun, Aned and Aethlem, and Arthur. Six are needed to control Drudwyn: Cors, Canastyr, Cilydd, Mabon, Dun-mane and Eidoel; and two—Dillus and Cyledyr—to control two unspecified whelps, possibly Aned and Aethlem. The list is completed by Gwyn's horse, the farcical Bwlch, Cyfwlch and Syfwlch to blow the horn, and Wrnach's sword for the kill. The emphasis laid on restraint may be significant. The tasks will be considered more fully in relation to their fulfilment, which does not accord with the details specified by the Giant.

We may now complete the poem *Pa Gur* from Chapter 3.3, which continues:

> Cei would plead with them while slaying them three at a time;
> When Celli is violated danger is experienced.
> Though Arthur was but playing, the blood was dripping
> In Afarnach's hall, in fighting with a hag;
> He slew dog-head in the dwelling of Dissernach;
> On Eidyn's mount he fought with champions,
> They fell a hundred at a time before Bedwyr strong of sinew;
> On the shores of Tryvrwyd in combat the Garwlwyd
> Victorious was his wrath with both sword and shield.

Cei thus battles with the three soul forces, but if the training of Celliwig is not observed at the Threshold, danger arises: i) in the skull, Afarnach's hall, where the blood must be displaced to form a clear mirror for thought; ii) amid the animalistic passions of 'doghead', the sub-race of the evil Balor of Ireland, whereas the astral forces are properly ordered in the realm of Dissernach/Diwrnach, who owns the cauldron of Irish treasures; iii) in the destructive will of Garwlwyd, a werewolf reputed to slay a man daily—but two on Saturdays so he need not slay on Sundays!

The next section displays Cei's strong moral qualities—he is presented as courageous, honourable, equable, powerful, energetic and persistent, so that 'unless it were God's act, Cei's death would not be achieved'. Finally we hear of his deeds:

> Worthy Cei and Llacheu used to fight in battles
> Before the pangs from blue-iron spears.
> On the top of Ystavingion Cei penetrated nine witches.
> Worthy Cei went to Mona to destroy a monster,
> His shield was a fragment against Palug's cat.
> When people shall ask who slew Palug's cat
> For whose food used to fall nine-score warriors...

Here the text breaks off, but probably only a line or two are missing, for after listing the helpers Cei's name has been mentioned seven times; Arthur has presented him fully to Glewlwyd as Guardian of the Threshold. Llacheu ('flashes') is Arthur's son, who is one of the three well-endowed (Triad 4) and fearless (Triad 9) men of the Island of Britain. (Incidentally, the remark that they fought before blue-iron spears supports Steiner's statement that the Arthurian mysteries began in the Bronze Age.) Experience on a mountain top had an important place in medieval initiations, as it had in the Gospels—the changed proportions of oxygen and nitrogen were there more suited to experience of the etheric world. This would help Cei's penetration of the nine 'witches', which may be taken as a euphemism for 'otherworldly female figures', the nine maidens referred to in *Preiddeu Annwn* who kindle the cauldron of the heavens and probably represent the divine Hierarchies. We shall have occasion to return later to the problems of Palug's cat, and of the nine-score warriors.

*   *   *   *   *

This completes the four experiences on the black-blue river which we related to the moon sphere. Nennius speaks of these four battles as being 'in the region Linnuis', a word interpreted as deriving from 'the people of Linden', related to Welsh 'llyn', a lake. The connection of the moon with water is well known.

Perhaps the most impressive artefacts found at sites ascribed to the Bronze Age are the large moon-shaped breast ornaments in gold called *lunulae*; and we may perhaps imagine that the candidate who completed successfully these four stages might at an annual ceremony have been invested with such an insignia.

6. On the Shallow River

With the sixth battle we can return to the specific guidance of Nennius as our main thread. This battle is 'on the river called "shallow" (Bassas)'. On the one hand the concept of shallowness suggests that we pass from a consciousness of objects to a consciousness of surfaces, a picture-consciousness such as we normally have today only in our dreams in a wholly subjective way. In past ages such a consciousness was well known in the form of atavistic clairvoyance, which did not yet stand over against a world of well-defined, sense-perceptible objects as we do, but yet illuminated from within the soul with a certain objectivity the constant flux of processes of growth and decay, both within the body and in nature. As this clairvoyance fell away it became increasingly chaotic. Thus when Culhwch first invoked his boon of Arthur, he did so in a motley mixture of characters where legend, history and whimsy were inseparably intertwined. The zany quality of some of these characters not only served to give the audience a good laugh, but also characterized the unreliability of such a consciousness, so long as it remains untutored. But now, after passing through the battles already described, which involved the 'know thyself' and the mastery of the giants, it becomes possible to approach this realm in a disciplined way.

On the other hand, a shallow river is proverbially fast-running, its surface constantly broken by ripples caused by all manner of irregularities breaking the surface, thus giving rise to the sparkling reflections of light which constantly flash up for a moment and disappear. This image captures accurately the quality of the picture-consciousness which now begins to appear. This swiftly-flowing stream points us also to the realm of Mercury, the winged messenger of the gods, who shines these flashes from his torch of soul-light into the black-blue moon region, and lifts us beyond it. (Mercury was considered before Venus because attention was paid to the frequency with which the planets appeared, not to any spatial positions that might be calculated.)

The corresponding picture in *Culhwch* occurs on the way back from the castle of Chief Giant Hawthorn, but before Arthur's court is reached. The party comes to the fort of the giant Wrnach, called (again) 'the greatest of forts in the world'. The conversation at the gate, too, is a mere copy of that which Culhwch had held with Glewlwyd: Wrnach is the representative of uncreative materialism. We learn that 'no guest has ever come from thence with his life'. The encounter takes place in three stages. No one but a craftsman (a worker with material substances) may enter; so Cei first gains entrance on his own as a furbisher of swords—he can transform the dulled sword of dead thinking into a living thinking shining with spirit, which none of Wrnach's men can do. By 'living thinking' is meant a thinking which does not only categorize plants under species, and examine parts of an uprooted specimen under a microscope, but follows in imagination the changing forces active in the growth of a plant as a totality in the course of the year, as it develops through alternate stages of expansion and contraction from seed to leaf and calyx, petals and pistils/stamens, fruit and seed; sensing the influences necessary for the transition from one stage to the next, what modifies the form of the whole according to habitat, and so on. It would also be concerned less, for example, with comparing isolated items dissected from different legends, and more with the dramatic sequences of each. For such a 'process-thinking' densification, fluidity, expansion and intensification become distinctive categories in much the same way as minerals, plants and animals are distinct for ordinary 'thing-thinking'. In such a way Cei burnishes 'half of one side' of Wrnach's sword.

Cei thus wins admission for Bedwyr, representing the will, the head of whose spear 'will leave its shaft, and draw blood from the wind, and settle upon the shaft again'—a fine picture for the way meditation awakens a new kind of willed thinking, vivid and vigorous, inwardly intense and no less saturated than sense-perception, which grasps the ever-mobile etheric world and draws it back into thought-forms.

There was something mysterious about the way Goreu 'and his comrades with him, as though it were nothing out of the way, crossed the three baileys until they came inside the fort'. Here the soul actually undergoes an extroversion comparable to that between sleeping and waking, and transposes itself into the qualitative essence of the world around it, expressed in the elements—though spiritually this occurs after, rather than before, Wrnach's death. Now Goreu can receive his name, and Arthur himself takes part in all further adventures.

Cei now points out to Wrnach that it is not his sword of thinking that is at fault, but the dead wood of the scabbard in which it has been constricted. He then takes the sword, and with it cuts of Wrnach's head—it is precisely enlivened thinking which, when properly furbished, overcomes the inadequacies of materialism's 'dead wood'.

* * * * *

We now need to consider the nature of the 'elements' which such a consciousness brings to the fore. We may start with the ordering derived from atavistic clairvoyance in folklore and fairy-tale thoughout the world, that of Cornwall providing a good example to hand.[14] Tin miners knew the 'knockers' or 'nuggies' whom they heard around the richest lodes, wizened, ungainly creatures the size of a baby, with large heads and faces of old men, who could be helpful, but became spiteful if their wishes were not respected. Fishermen threw back offerings to the 'bucca' (English 'puck') whom they believed could lead them to a good catch. Country folk told of the 'piskies', spirits of hills, groves and rivers, who occasionally enticed people into a beautiful underground world, or bestowed the power to heal by touch; and of the 'spriggans', held responsible for storms, who changed size at will, and were to be seen as grotesque warriors near cairns, cromlechs and barrows. There were also dancing flames of white, red or blue on the moors, 'Jack o' Lantern' or 'Joan the Wad', who misled wayfarers by night. Such lore thus speaks of categories of subordinate but lively beings within the framework of nature.

It is obvious that these categories are absolutely fundamental, from the fact that we need to eat, drink, breathe and warm ourselves, and divide the products of digestion in the same way. An ancient science recognized them in a more precise, qualitative way: densification rather than 'earth'; fluidity, such as that of colour, rather than 'water'; expansiveness rather than 'air'; and a qualitative moral warmth. Early Greek philosophers such as Thales and Heraclitus, who built their philosophies on these four elements, and Galen who founded his medical study of the temperaments upon them, were not simple-minded, but were concerned with an aspect of the totality of existence different from that which is generally considered today.

In northern Europe the beings of the elements were studied primarily as the craftsmen of nature, and the Tintagel area was particularly well adapted to this. Greek science conceived the earth element as cold and dry, which could be well experienced on the headland in winter, especially in the mysterious 'tunnel' (Plate 1). Water, cold and wet, could be only too easily experienced as such in the cave beneath. Air, thought of as warm and moist, was exceptionally so in St Nectan's Glen, as spray drifted across from the waterfall. And fire, warm and dry, was exemplified near the carvings in Rocky Valley, where the very rock also contains pyrites (Greek: fire). At the centre of balance we find Bossiney mound, 'the place of the bold chief', representing the Greek 'quintessence', i.e., the ascent to a higher synthesis.

Turning again to *Culhwch*, we shall not be surprised to find that the next episodes relate to these elements. The first task is to obtain Eidoel from imprisonment on a *rocky crag*, and he is soon handed over by his captor Glini who offers support: after the fifth battle the temptations of earthly matter are soon overcome.

Next comes the freeing of Mabon, prisoner from time immemorial, taken from his mother when three nights old. Mabon son of Modron derives from the Latin Maponus, a youth god, son of Matrona, a mother goddess. Several heads of Maponus have been found along Hadrian's wall, where he seems to have been revered by the legions as a form of Apollo, but his significance remains unclear. The search for him incorporates the world-wide story of 'the oldest animal'. Cei, Bedwyr, Gwrhyr (the Interpreter) and Eidoel, Mabon's cousin, question the ouzel, stag, owl and eagle in turn, without success. They can do this because at this level of consciousness the group soul of each species can be perceived and resembles a man[8]. Only when Cei and Gwrhyr are carried by *water* on the shoulders of the salmon—the fish of wisdom—to the wall of Gloucester, is the prisoner identified through his lamentations. Supported by Arthur and his men on land, Cei breaks the wall and carries Mabon off on the salmon's back. We have here the important picture that the imprisoned youth-god is freed by water through the salmon of wisdom and the effort of Cei. 'Arthur came home and Mabon with him, a free man.' Only after the three giants have been overcome is freedom achieved: the spirit has hitherto been prisoner of the body since 'three nights old'.

The central episode of this group tells how a bitch and her two whelps are surrounded and 'changed back by God to their human semblance for Arthur'. We shall revert to the question of shape-shifting shortly, but meanwhile note the hint of redemptive forces which bring the one-sidedness of the animal back into human balance. This is appropriate to the quintessence.

The next item concerns an ant-hill, an image of the stage at which thinking has become so alive, in the sense described above, that thoughts relate to one another out of their intrinsic nature as if they were ants.[15] Victor son of Scorcher saves the ant-hill from *fire* by his sword, and in gratitude the ants collect the flax seed required for the wedding veil, 'and the lame ant brought in the last seed before night'. Thus the veil can be completed, the veil of physical sense-existence can be finished with.

Cei is finally involved in an episode starting 'in the highest *wind* in the world,' whence drifting smoke identifies Dillus. To make a leash out of his beard whilst he lives (to turn living thought to practical account in controlling the animal impulses) Cei digs a pit whilst Dillus sleeps, tumbles him in, cuts the beard, and then kills him—but does not receive the praise he expects.

* * * * *

In *Owein*, in the midst of a vale like a great waterway, is a great tree 'with the tips of its branches greener than the greenest fir trees. And under that tree is a fountain, and beside the fountain is a marble slab, and on the slab there is a silver bowl fastened to a silver chain'. Such a tree and fountain figure in many an Irish tale. In the past men felt the earth as a great living organism, whose life—expressed in the rhythms of day and night, the lunar months and the year—gushed up into their own bodies like a fountain. They felt their inner being as a sculptor who moulds this fountain of life-forces to create in childhood their physical appearance, to shape the brain and to kindle the digestive processes; and then to mould their speech, temperament and particular way of thinking. Finally, after the convulsion referred to above, they experienced these forces directly in living Imaginative pictures, which are represented by the specially green leaves at the tips of the tree.

The experience of such Imaginations is naturally different from our ordinary consciousness. What it is like we may learn from poems ascribed to Taliesin probably written in the tenth or eleventh century. For example in *Cad Goddeu*[9] we have many lines such as:

> I have been in many shapes before I attained congenial form...
> I have been a drop in the air, I have been a shining star...
> I have journeyed as an eagle, I have been a boat on the sea...

The list is haphazard, and the despair of commentators. What was the poet up to? Sixteen metamorphoses in all are mentioned: swordblade, drop, star, word; book, light, bridge, eagle; boat, general, string, sword; shield, harpstring, poker, tree. There is a similar haphazard list in the *Hanes Taliesin*, related to the time when Gwion was still in the elemental world before birth: frog, crow, chain, roe; wolf-cub, wolf, thrush, fox; martin, squirrel, antler, iron; spearhead, bull, boar, grain. Again sixteen! This is the only fact one can at first get hold of. May it not be that something is being conveyed through this very fact, in a typically obscure druidic manner?

This form of consciousness within the world of the elements, which consists in continual self-transformation (shape-shifting), actually depends on the development of the organ known as the sixteen-petal lotus flower, situated in the larynx. This gives the ability to enter into and become one with world processes without knowing how they are connected with one another, which is precisely the quality of these strange lists. The means of developing this organ received classical expression in the Eightfold Path of the Buddha: significant views, controlled aims, considered speech, harmonious actions, moderated living, idealistic effort, learning from experience, and contemplative review of life. An explanation in modern terms has been given by Rudolf Steiner.[10]

Moreover, the soul which experiences itself in these transformations is alive outside, and no longer inside, the body—as Taliesin's examples state. This reaches its culmination in a later poem in the *Hanes Taliesin* in such lines as:

> I have been in the galaxy at the throne of the Distributor...

I have been fostered in the land of the Deity...
I was with my Lord in the highest sphere...

It is in this sense that the word 'extroversion' was used, a pouring out into the world around.

The 'shallow river' thus points to the burnishing of thinking and its gradual transformation into Imaginative consciousness, in which pictures flash up from living within the world of the elements. But this is not yet enough to know how what flashes up is connected with other events in the world of reality. A further step must be taken.

7. In Celidon Wood

The seventh battle was 'in the wood of Celidon, that is, cat coed Celidon'. Commentators are confident that this refers to the Caledonian forest of the Scottish border. But, if this is so obvious, why does Nennius take the trouble to repeat just this one phrase in Welsh? May it not be that he seeks to warn: this is used as a technical terms, not literally? 'Celidon' could mean 'heavenly ocean'. What else do we know of it?

It was to Celidon that Myrddin withdrew after the battle of Arfderydd, said to have been 'brought about by the cause of a lark's nest' (Triad 84), a typical bardic euphemism for a spiritual centre striving up to the source of celestial song. According to one poem, 'To no one has been shown in one hour of dawn (a special time for meditating on the sun) what was revealed to Myrddin, seven score and seven delicious apple trees of equal height, length and size, which sprang from the bosom of mercy... The delicious apple tree, with blossom of pure white and wide spreading branches, produces sweet apples for those who can digest them. And they have always grown in the wood which grows apart' (*Afallenau*). Can this be the wood of Celidon?

Myrddin hides in such a tree, 'fruit-bearing, of great value, famous', whose 'peculiar power' makes it invisible to his pursuers. He bemoans the loss of leaves and food as winter comes on. Found at length, he is enticed to court only by the music of the lute, but returns to the wood, where for ten and twenty years he 'endures sickness and grief'. His twin sister, the queen, builds there for him an observatory with seventy doors and seventy windows and encourages him to 'open the books of inspiration without fear'. He studies Phoebus (the sun), Venus and the stars, and 'the pale wanderer foretells the tidings which will come'. This sounds more like research into megalithic star-wisdom by means of a wooden reproduction of a circle of trilithons, than the madness usually pictured. He said of himself 'I was taken out of myself, I was as a spirit, and knew the history of people long past, and could foretell the future. I knew then the secrets of nature, bird flight, star wanderings, and the way fish glide.' (*Vita Merlini*). For Myrddin at least, Celidon wood was the source of inspiration for his poetry and prophecies. He advised his followers: 'Attend, little pig—thou initiated pig—burrow not with thy snout on the top of the hill, but in a secret hiding place among the forests' (*Oinau*).

It was also in Celidon wood that Drystan and Essyllt (Trystan and Iseult) experienced their love together, whilst yet remaining chaste. Drystan, son of Tallorc ('first boar'), was one of the Three Powerful Swineherds from whom Arthur failed to steal even a pig.[16] This strange story simply means he had qualified in the pig mysteries. Elsewhere Arthur was asked[17] to judge whether Essyllt should go to king Mark or to Drystan, and offered Mark the choice of having her when the trees bore leaves or when they were bare. His mind on the long winter evenings, Mark chose the latter; whereupon Essyllt broke into a song of praise for Arthur and for the holly, ivy and yew, which retain their leaves—Drystan was hers.

The motif here is one of chaste love, that which survives the fall of the leaves, and the discomfiture of Mark, who with his asses' ears was another representative of the intellect.

Turning now to *Culhwch*, we find that when Cei, who has led every adventure up to this point, takes to Arthur the leash made from Dillus' beard, Arthur bursts into a song, in terms which seem to criticize Cei for having killed Dillus. Cei is so enraged that he will have nothing more to do with Arthur 'in his hour of need from that time forward'. We shall have occasion to observe that in every story Cei turns back at this precise point for one reason or another. The wood of Celidon cannot be entered by the faculty of thinking, but demands a metamorphosis of the feelings, such as that of Drystan and Essyllt. A fourteenth-century manuscript explains that Arthur had been suckled as an infant by Cei's mother, thus depriving Cei of the forces of the heart.

But it is the tale of *Owein* which here becomes specific. The hero has been told: 'Beside the tree and the fountain is a marble slab, with a bowl fastened by a silver chain. Throw a bowlful of water over the slab, and you will hear a great peal of thunder, and there will be an icy shower of hailstones, and not one leaf will be left on the tree. Thereupon a flight of birds will alight on the tree, and never yet have you heard in your own country a song so delightful as they will sing. And when you are most enraptured, you will hear a great panting and groaning approaching along the valley, and a knight in black upon a black horse will fall on you as briskly as he can . . .' And so it happens.

This expresses accurately the fact that in order to progress, all the Imaginative pictures acquired with so much effort at the previous stage must now be suppressed by active forgetting (the tree loses every leaf), so that consciousness becomes quite empty, without falling asleep.[18] (Myrddin and Essyllt were both aware of this.) Then out of the silence a real sounding from the objective spiritual world (the bird song) begins to be heard as Inspiration. The pupil is no longer 'in his own country', i.e. in the body. And there is the continuing hazard that if the soul-activity is not strong enough it will be swamped by dark forces rising from the lower nature (the black knight in the valley). Cynon, who first tells this tale, is defeated by the black knight and forced to return home ignominiously; Cei and others in Arthur's party who arrive later are also defeated. Only those with a mature feeling life—Owein, Gwalchmei and Arthur himself—can go further.

A somewhat similar picture is found in the Apocalypse, at the transition from the seals (which are visual, like the leaves) to the trumpets (which are audible). There is silence in heaven, the casting down of the altar fire (the hail), peals of thunder, and an earthquake (the groaning in the valley). We shall subsequently meet other pictures of this 'perilous passage', which is never without pain.

Owein gives the black knight a mortal blow to the brain (eliminates his thoughts) and pursues him to the gate of a great shining city. The knight enters, but the portcullis descends on Owein, so that his horse is cut in two behind him and the inner gate closes in front. The point is reached where it is no longer possible to turn back—sometimes described as the Water Trial. He is trapped, were it not for the selfless love of another, springing from 'the bosom of mercy'.

As a melody lies not in the notes as such but in the relationships between them, so at this level it is not the Imaginations which again begin to arise that bring understanding, but the Inspirations flowing in the relationships between them. For example, the visible rays of the stars vanish, but there comes forth from between them the revelation of the spirits, the gods, through the music of the spheres and the speech of the cosmic Word. Man becomes fully orientated in his primal nature, which is spread out like the 'spreading branches' over the whole surrounding world as far as the planets, where he knows himself to live between death and rebirth. His view thus extends beyond the single life to 'the history of peoples'. Only his earthly body is now 'outside' him.

Such a consciousness requires a particular background to reflect it.[19] At the time when Tintagel was founded this was the element of water—even the temples of Egypt were clustered near the Nile. When the initiate looked into river or sea he could see secrets that endure; in the drifting mist or downpouring rain he beheld secrets related to transient things. We remarked in Chapter 2.4 that Tintagel was in this respect peculiarly well and diversely equipped. Later the air element generally provided the required background—hence Greek temples are usually in the mountains, but the one which remained in connection with Hyperborea, Tempe, was situated by the river Pinios, as in earlier times.

Celidon wood is thus the special wood in which the leaves of Imagination are shed and replaced by the sweet singing of Inspirations from the heavenly ocean, the wood which grows apart. 'The steward (i.e., Cei), approaching it, will not succeed in obtaining its fine fruit . . . Sweet apple tree, a red-flowered tree, which grows hidden in the forest of Celyddon, though it be sought it will be in vain owing to its peculiar quality . . .' (*Afallenau*).

8. A Ritual Miscarries

Medrawd, whose name may be interpreted metaphorically as 'understanding', was in early Welsh tradition a person of valour and courtesy, also known as Maelgwas 'a princely youth' or Melwys, son of Baeddon, 'Noble Pig son of Little Boar'. In Cornish the names became Modret and Melwas, Latinized by Geoffrey as Modredus, English Mordred. A late Triad names him as one of the three kingly knights, whose dispositions were so placid and mild and pure in discourse that it was hard for anyone to refuse what they wanted.

But Triad 54 tells us that 'when in Arthur's absence Medrawd came to Arthur's court at Celliwig in Cornwall, he left neither meat nor drink that he did not consume, and he pulled Gwenhwyvar from her throne, and then struck a blow upon her.' The sequel is described in Caradoc of Llancarvan's *Life of Gildas*[20] (written before Geoffrey's *History*): 'Glastonia was besieged by the tyrant Arthur with a countless multitude on account of his wife Guennuvar, whom the wicked king Melwas had violated and carried off and brought there for protection . . . When he saw that war was prepared the abbot of Glastonia . . . stepped in between the contending armies, and in peaceable manner advised his king Melwas to restore the ravished lady in peace and goodwill'.

Another late Triad lists Medrawd as one of the three dishonoured men of the island of Britain. 'For when Arthur left the government of Britain in his custody whilst he marched against the Roman emperor, Medrawd took the crown from Arthur by usurpation and seduction: and in order to keep it he confederated with the Saxons; and on this account the Cambrians lost the throne of England . . . ' The entry in the *Annales Cambriae* for 538 which reads: 'The battle of Camlann in which Arthur and Medrawd were slain; and there was death in England and Ireland', suggests that he also drew to his aid the Irish invaders known to have landed in NE Cornwall in the sixth century.

The questions must arise why the noble youth turned against Arthur in this way. An interesting document going back to the thirteenth century suggests that this might be due to a moon-initiation controlled by Cei, which went wrong. What follows collates the two extant versions translated by M. Williams [21] and also draws on her commentary and character-identification (C = Cei, M = Melwas, G = Gwenhwyvar):

C: Who is the man who sits in the common part of the feast
Without for him either its beginning or its end,
Seated down there below the hall?

M: Melwas from the Isle of Glass.
Thou with the gilded caskets—
I have drunk none of thy wine.

The initiation scene is represented as a banqueting hall, Cei as hierophant sitting at high table with the caskets of knowledge. Below the lesser grades sit those who, whilst admitted past the threshold, do not receive the wine, representing the blood, the essential bodily forces. Reference to the Isle of Glass, before it became identified with Glastonbury, may claim some experience of the otherworld.

M: Black is my steed and trusty beneath me
   And because of water he will not fear,
   And before no man will he turn aside.

G: Green is my steed, of the tint of leaves.
   He is completely despised, he is no man
   Who does not fulfil his word.

The black steed of the intellect is a trusty support in the physical world, and is not frightened to enter the elemental world; but this, in fact, requires the green steed of living thinking (Chapter 3.6), and with it must go the step in morality, the fulfilment of one's word.

C: Wait a little. . . I do not pour out my wine
   For a man who cannot hold out in the fray.

G: In the forefront of the fray
   No man can hold out but Cei the Tall son of Sevin.
   He would not stand up to Cei in his wine.

M: I would wade a ford even if it were a fathom deep
   With a coat of mail, on the shore of the ebb.
   I am the man to stand up to Cei.

The neophyte must be tested at the Threshold, the shore of the tide. Melwas wants to enter the watery realm of the elemental world with physical armour, despite the danger of it drowning him; but the physical should not be carried across the Threshold.

G: Silence, lad, silence your wild talk.
   If you are no better than you appear
   You would not stand up to Cei as one of eight.

M: Gwenhwyvar of the silvery glance,
   Do not reject me although I am young;
   I would myself stand up to a hundred.

Gwenhwyvar, meaning 'white phantom', represents the moon-goddess 'of the silvery glance'. She distinguishes reality from appearance, an ability depending on the two-petal lotus (see Chapter 3.2), which is crucial when the physical bodily senses are no longer available to assist judgment. She throws him back on himself, enjoining the silencing of his personal aspirations, in order to make possible the step to Inspiration (Chapter 3.7). To stand against a hundred is to separate from the crowd, a real test in early medieval times and unachieved by many even today. Melwas stands his ground with becoming modesty as to his inexperience.

> G: Pshaw, lad of black and yellow!
>   With your head red like lungs you are unlike Cei in size.
>   It is a drunken man's nature to be weak.
>
> M: We will therefore keep to what is right.
>   I am Melwas, let us leave it at that.

Gwenhwyvar again taunts him as lily-livered and inebriated. He is not drawn, and in a dignified way asserts the 'I am'.

> C: Since you have begun, go on with your conversation.
>
> G: A lad knows who fondles him . . .
>   After gazing long at your appearance
>   I thought I had seen you before this.
>
> M: Gwenhwyvar of the rejecting glance,
>   Tell me if you know where before now you saw me.
>
> G: I saw a man of moderate size
>   At a long table in the land of Dyfneint
>   Serving wine to his friends.
>
> M: Gwenhwyvar of pleasant speech,
>   Vain words are natural from a woman's mouth.
>   There you did see me.

The opening was proverbial in Welsh: 'a lad knows who fondles him, but does not know who loves him'. In the ancient mysteries it was the neophyte's place to answer questions, as occurs in the alternative text, not to ask them. (This did not begin until the time of Parzival.) Reference to Dyfneint (Devon and Cornwall) suggests that Melwas had been knighted (a man of moderate size) at Arthur's court, and should have known this. The present moon-initiation obviously occurs elsewhere. Cei must have smiled at Melwas' mistakes:

M: I hate the smile of an old grey-haired man
With his sword like a skewer beneath his chin,
Who desires but cannot achieve.

C: Still more hateful to me a proud man, timid except in words
Who will not be silent, nor draw his sword.

M: Take that!

C: *You* take that!

Melwas loses his self-control and provokes Cei, the skewer suggesting that the latter, who turns back before achievement, is mere steward of Arthur's court. The brawl must mean his rejection.

This may well be sufficient reason for him to have turned against Arthur. He stands as an example of ordinary thinking, initially honourable, which tries to master the spirit unchanged, fails, and turns against it.

CHAPTER FOUR

TRIALS OF THE SPIRIT

1. In White Castle

Whereas previous battles have taken place in 'nature', the eighth is 'in White Castle' (Guinnion). This we may take as the shining sphere of the sun. Turning first to *Culhwch*, we find this confirmed in that Arthur first seeks Precious White, the whelp of Fire. The latter is held prisoner by Gwyn, son of Nudd ('white son of the mist'), along with others including Creiddylad (Cordelia), daughter of Lludd (Lear) Silver-Hand. Cordelia ('the most majestic maiden who ever was in the islands of Britain') had been going with Gwythyr, son of Greidawl (Victor son of Scorcher), when Gwyn carried her off by force, so Gwythyr had come to fight for her. Arthur set free all Gwyn's prisoners, and ruled that Cordelia remain with her father, Gwyn and Gwythyr to fight for her each Mayday until doomsday. This is widely regarded as a version of the Persephone myth, Gwyn and Gwythyr representing the forces of winter and summer respectively. An interesting ancient gloss[1] said 'As Michael was Angel of the Hebrews, so was Gwythyr of the Celts'. It was Gwythyr who had saved the ants from fire (Chapter 3.6). The name Gwyn is a transliteration of the Irish Finn, to whom are assigned many poems on the theme of summer and winter, and we saw in Chapter 2.3 how important was this sun-rhythm of life in an earlier age whose fruits were to be carried into later times.

Indeed, mock battles between summer and winter were enacted at many places in Britain at Beltane (Mayday) and Samhain (1 Nov) right up until this century.

Arthur next obtained the steed Brown Mane and the leash of Cors. He then went to Brittany to seek the dogs of Gluttonous the Breton; to Ireland to seek Gwrgi Seferi and the King of Ireland's son (none of these four actually asked for by the Giant); then to the North to catch Cyledyr the Wild (whom Gwyn had compelled to eat his father's heart). He is thus depicted as circling round Britain as the sun circles the zodiac; and since he became involved, the five adventures of Cei have thus been extended by seven to twelve in all.

We now return to *Owein*, where the hero was trapped in the portcullis of a 'great shining city'. But a maiden approaches and gives out of compassion the ring of invisibility, on the grounds that 'hadst thou a lady-love, best of lovers wouldst thou be'. When the black knight's followers come for him he can therefore elude them. We need to confront here the idea of invisibility, which keeps cropping up in so many tales, yet strikes ordinary thinking as so impossible. The initiate at this stage unites spiritually with the object of his contemplation to such an extent that he loses temporarily his separate spiritual identity, and thus becomes invisible, he 'wears the mantle of Arthur', as did Myrddin. This is clearly expressed by St Paul in I Corinthians ii:15, in the words: 'On the one hand the spiritual man discerns all things, he on the other is discerned by no one'; although the word 'discern' is paraphrased out by translators to whom this experience is unknown. The story of the 'faery castle' (Chapter 1.4) tells us that once in summer and once in winter the knights forming the community of the Round Table at Tintagel entered this level of consciousness, and hence became invisible to the 'peasants' and 'local folk' whose atavistic clairvoyance enabled them to perceive the fact.

The maiden, with yellow curling hair and a gold headband, leads Owein to her own chamber, where 'there was not one panel without its different kind of golden image thereon', and washes, shaves and feeds him. When the funeral of the black knight passes, he catches sight of the Lady of the Fountain, 'and when he beheld the Lady he was fired with love of her in all his parts. "God knows" said the maiden "she loves not thee, neither a little nor at all!" ' However, she agrees to 'go a-wooing' for him to her mistress, and after interchanges full of humour, he is in due course presented to the Lady in a mantle bordered with gold thread, and buskins with the image of a gold lion. They are married with the people's agreement, and Owein defends the fountain for three years. This whole passage is distinguished not only by the golden glow of the sun but also by the sensitive descriptions of the maiden's selfless love for Owein, his love for the Lady, her grief at the death of her lover, and her love of the maiden. We realize that the sun is the source not only of light and life, but also of love.[2]

Meanwhile Arthur becomes concerned at Owein's absence, sets out to find him, and reaches the fountain. Owein, defending it as the black knight, throws each of Arthur's knights who approaches (Cei twice), until only Gwalchmei and Arthur remain. Owein and Gwalchmei fight for the usual three days, until the latter's helmet is turned and Owein recognizes him; they embrace in noble loving regard. Thereupon Arthur and his court are welcomed and feasted for three months.

* * * * *

At this eighth battle, according to Nennius, 'Arthur carried on his shoulders an image of St Mary Ever Virgin, and there was great slaughter of "them" through the strength of Our Lord Jesus Christ and of the holy Mary his maiden mother.' This evidences a Mariolatry quite foreign to the Celtic church, and was probably added after the submission to Rome. The *Annales Cambriae* retains what is probably closer to the original text: 'Arthur carried the cross of Our Lord Jesus Christ on his shield for three days and nights, and the Britons were victorious'; although the connection of this with the battle of Badon is a thought to be another late interpolation.

It is our thesis that the Arthurian mysteries existed at least a millenium before Christ. St Augustine (354-430) and other early Fathers also believed that followers of Christ were to be found even before His descent to earth, although they were not called Christians.[3] This is further confirmed by the tradition that Christianity was first brought to Britain by Bran the Blessed (Chapter 2.2). Rudolf Steiner described this situation as follows:[4] 'Up to the time of the Mystery of Golgotha, Christ had been a Sun Being, had belonged to the sun. The knights of the Round Table stood on these rocks (at Tintagel), gazed at the interplay between spirits born of the sun and the earth-born spirits, and felt that the forces living in this play of nature spirits poured into their hearts and above all through their etheric bodies. Therewith they received into themselves the Christ impulse which was streaming away from the sun, and was living in everything that is brought into being by the sun forces.'

We find this further confirmed in the *Black Book of Carmarthen* in the lines: 'Thou, sun; to him intercession and vows are made, Lord, heavenly Christ, the pillar of beneficence'; and in the *Red Book of Hergest*: 'Christ Jesus, who art in complete possession of light . . . Christ the mystery one.' The Greeks too were well aware that reverence was paid to the sun-spirit in pre-Christian Britain (Chapter 2.2). In the autumn, Apollo, who led the spiritual sun-forces working through the elements, left Delphi for his primeval home in the north-west: as the physical sun moves south, the spiritual sun moves north. The will of Apollo could thus be read where specially chosen stones withheld the physical sun rays, but allowed the spiritual rays of life and love to penetrate.

What then was the name of this Sun Spirit in Britain? A reference in the sixteenth-century manuscript *Barddas*,[5] which purports to record ancient bardic tradition, but is suspected by some scholars of being a fabrication, gives the link: 'Hu the Mighty—Jesus son of God—the least in respect of worldly greatness whilst in the flesh, the greatest in heaven of all visible majesties'. A poem in the name of Taliesin speaks of 'the ethereal one with the rainbow girdle, Hu with the extended wings, sovereign of heaven.' And a fifteenth-century poet, Rhy Brydydd, says more clearly:

> The smallest, if compared with small
> Is the mighty Hu in the world's judgment,
> And he is the greatest, and Lord over us,
> And our God of Mystery:
> Light is his course, and swift:
> A particle of lucid sunshine is his car:
> He is great on land and sea,
> The greatest whom I shall behold—
> Greater than worlds. Let us beware
> Of mean indignity to Him who deals in bounty.

Steiner confirms this connection in his remark:[6] 'The Mystery of Golgotha was received with deep understanding in the European mysteries. In the mysteries of Wales and Britain . . . the initiates realized in full clarity that he whom they had sought as Hu had come to earth as Christ.'

The descent of Christ from the Godhead, through the sun, to become man on earth, obviously made a great change in what could be perceived in the light flowing from the sun, and what could be perceived amidst the earthly elements. Steiner said of this:[4] 'Christ died cosmically from the sun to the earth . . . If in the first five centuries men looked out over the sea, and had been prepared by the exercises practised by the twelve around Arthur, who were concerned above all with the mysteries of the zodiac, they could not merely see the play of nature, but they could begin to read a meaning in it . . . And when they deciphered it, they read the spiritual fact of the Mystery of Golgotha . . . This represented, as it were, the science of the higher graduates of King Arthur's Round Table.'

* * * * *

The corresponding verse in *Priddeu Annwn* speaks on the one hand of 'the quartered fort', meaning the heart, and on the other of 'the island of the radiant door'. Sparkling was here the drink, where the polarity of light and darkness was created. The sun is an 'island' in the whole sphere apparently travelled by the sun around the earth. But on the path of initiation, and on the path of the soul after death, the sun marks the transition between the Soul World and Spiritland. It is indeed the 'radiant door' to Spiritland.

The seven stages of the Soul World have been described and named by Rudolf Steiner in his fundamental book entitled *Theosophy*. These stages can now be recognized in the seven 'Battles' we have described so far (excluding the first, which is no longer experienced today). 'Glowing Desires' for material enjoyment can no longer be satisfied, and are burnt up by the mastiff on the Plain of Death. 'Flowing Sensitivity' has to find a single focus to pass the Gatekeeper. 'Wishes' must give way to the demands of destiny insisted upon by Olwen. 'Sympathies and Antipathies' lying at the core of the soul have to become organs of discernment in the presence of the Threefold Giant. 'Soul Light' begins to shine through the furbishing of thinking to Imagination. 'Active Soul Force' is needed to defeat the black knight and penetrate to Celidon wood where the Inspirations begin to resound. And now 'Soul Life' stirs as the sun sphere is experienced. These are the seven stages of preperation through which all who proceed further to investigate the spiritual world must 'come back up'.

We now follow the Arthurian path into Spiritland, where four more stages are indicated; a further three stages in higher spiritland lie beyond any texts available for commentary. This realm differs qualitatively from what has gone before, and is more difficult to depict and interpret. We shall, however, become able to see how the Grail path differs from the Arthurian, and gain some idea of the path of the soul returning to a new incarnation.

2. The City of the Legions (Gereint)

The ninth battle is 'in the city of the Legions'. We might imagine that the British, having taken over the camp of their former enemies, the Romans, are now assailed by the Saxons. Our attention is drawn to the polarity, for they are very different enemies—the Romans victors of Europe, well-disciplined and organized, expanding a highly developed but materialized culture; and the Saxons marauding bands, destructive and rapacious, largely illiterate but full of individual courage. Both represent Mars, god of war.

We shall understand the situation here best by considering first the story of 'Gereint, son of Erbin' in the *Mabinogion*. This looks at first like two separate stories with interlude and epilogue. The first half concerns combat with a single very large knight, the second half with a total of exactly one-hundred knights, of whom the principal one is very small.

Gereint rides unarmed with Gwenhwyvar from Caerleon ('the Fort of the Legions'!) towards a hunt led by Arthur for a special stag (see Chapter 2.2)—pure white, presumptious and exceeding majestical. They encounter a knight, and 'certain were they that they had never seen man and armour more remarkable for size'. His dwarf responds to enquiries, first from Gwenhwyvar's maid and then from Gereint, with a whip across the face that draws blood. Gereint, unarmed, can but follow the knight to Cardiff, where a tournament is in preparation. He lodges with an impoverished earl who once owned the city, with his wife, and only daughter Enid. They provide him with arms, and he vanquishes 'the knight of the sparrow-hawk' whom he had followed. This knight proves to be Edern (Ider, Chapter 3.5) son of Nudd and brother of Gwyn (Chapter 4.1), and he seems to hold a position at Arthur's court comparable to Loki among the Norse gods. When Edern, in a state of collapse, is sent to Gwenhwyvar to apologize, Arthur grieves to see 'a youth so excellent' in such a state. Enid is then brought to court by Gereint in her modest shift, is richly clothed by Gwenhwyvar, and is presented with the head of the white hart killed by Arthur himself. They marry and sleep in Arthur's own bedchamber.

After three happy years Gereint is called by his ageing father to his Cornish estate. Gereint's love for Enid is such that at length his retinue begin to scoff at his becoming soft. Enid's deep concern at this he mistakes for faithlessness, and he sets out full of jealousy, bidding her lead her horse ahead of him in silence. Three times she breaks silence to warn him of attack, and is made to lead first three, then seven, and finally twelve captured horses. After a night in the forest, when he makes her keep watch, a lad finds them food and lodging. The local earl calls, and plans with Enid to abduct her, but again she warns Gereint, and they depart by night, leaving the horses in payment (a detail rarely mentioned). The earl follows with fourscore knights, but Gereint throws each of them in succession.

They now cross a bridge, and Gereint is induced to lie that 'I did not know the road is forbidden to any'. Challenged by the Little King, 'it was ugly for Gereint to do battle, so very small was he'. At length he strikes the king on the head to the bone, and grants quarter on condition that if the Little King hears of him being in distress, he will come to his aid. Gereint, sorely wounded himself, declines hospitality and is resting, when Cei comes upon and attacks him, but Gereint nevertheless throws him. Cei then sends Gwalchmei, who after an encounter recognizes him and advises him to come to court to be healed. When Gereint declines, Gwalchmei sends to Arthur to move his court onto the road, so that Gereint and Enid arrive there unwittingly and are detained.

As soon as possible Gereint is on his way again with Enid. He confronts and slays three giants, but his wounds reopen, and 'when he saw Enid he fell to the ground for dead, from his horse'. An earl responds to Enid's cry, and takes them to his hall; but after an altercation he boxes her ear, and she cries out again. At this, Gereint rises up as if from the dead to slay the earl, to the terror of all present. The Little King comes up, and provides hospitality and healing.

Finally Gereint leads them all to the court of earl Ywein, where enchanted games take place within a hedge of mist, from which no man returns. Ywein offers to stop the games, but Gereint enters the mist and reaches an orchard and an open pavilion. When he sits beside a maiden he is challenged by a knight, whom he duly vanquishes. He sounds the horn hanging on an apple tree, the mist disappears, and all return home in peace.

This tale expresses a fundamental moral conception of the Arthurian mysteries, according to which good and evil are not polar opposites, but good is the condition of unstable balance between two different kinds of evil. The overlarge knight, proud and arrogant, lives in the wind and clouds—the realm of the sparrowhawk—as well as in human souls. It is only through his avowal of the modest Enid that Gereint defeats this figure, known to Anthroposophy as Lucifer;[7] he stands for selfishness and disregard for others (the flick of the whip). Nevertheless he is regarded as 'so excellent', because as son of the king of the otherworld he carries the moon-wisdom of the past (this whole section is under the aegis of Gwenhwyvar, the moon-figure), and is also the inspirer of art, which should lift humanity above material things, and is good so long as not carried to excess.

The second part of the tale is centred on the Little King, known to Anthroposophy as Ahriman. He lives in the hardening forces within the earth, which rise into human etheric bodies, and can make the innumerable, unmastered earthly passions and desires (the one-hundred opponents) take on human form in the soul.[8] He is the expression of lying, destructive impulses, and all that seeks to fetter man to the earth for future ages; but mastery of the clarity and precision he gives to thinking is a necessary part of the process of redemption of the earth.

The final section shows how, when Gereint has 'died' and come to life again, thus bearing the forces of resurrection, he is able to break down the hedge of mist which separates the sense-world from the other world. It was through Christ's descent into hell, the realm of the Little King, that He brought the power which will transform the earth once again into spirit.

In *Culhwch*, too, we are now presented with two different pictures of these two opponents: that of a sharp pointed tusk, and that of a rounded cauldron. Arthur next goes after White Tusk Chief Boar, whose tusk is required to 'shave' the Giant. He takes with him Mabon son of Lightning (possibly the Mabon of Chapter 3.6), and the whelp Precious White, the sun forces acquired in Chapter 4.1. It is with the help of Arthur's mare and his dog that Cadw ('keep') kills the boar. Only animal (astral) forces purified by the sun can vanquish the sharp tusk.

Here too follows an interlude, during which Menw is sent to check that Twrch Trwyth still has the treasures for which he is to be hunted, and is scathed by the latter's poison. The wisdom which he represents may yet be distorted and rejected.

Arthur then embarks for Ireland in his ship, White Form (the purified astral body), to acquire the cauldron of Diwrnach, or Di-Wrnach, the opposite of Wrnach (Chapter 3.6), perhaps suggesting a theology which has rigidified in dogma, as the opposite of materialism. The original cauldron of Irish legend was brought from heaven by the goddess Dana herself, and no one came from it unsatisfied. The *Thirteen Treasures of the Island of Britain*[9] include the cauldron of Dyrnwch the Giant which 'if meat for a coward were put in it to boil, it would never boil; but if meat for a brave man, it would boil quickly' (and thus distinguish the brave from the cowardly). This is clearly the dark blue cauldron with pearls around its rim referred to in *Priddeu Annwn* (Chapter 2.5). Such a cauldron, 'filled with the treasures of Ireland', can only be understood as the bowl of the night sky and the stars, whose inhabitants provide man's true spiritual nourishment, judge his deeds after death, and prepare with him his new incarnation. This was expressed in the wisdom of the past, rigidified into theology which must now be gained anew as individual experience. Bedwyr, representing the will, simply seizes the cauldron (grasps the cosmos in Intuition), whilst Llenlleawg swings Arthur's sword in a circle (follows the sun round the sky) to rout Diwrnach and his host. Mastery of the Hibernian mysteries was necessary before encountering Twrch Trwyth.

This picture of finding the right relation to the surface of the earth, between the rounded forces of the cosmos and the sharp attacks from sub-earthly realms, the balance between 'too much' and 'too little', in twelfth-century Wales the path between *traha* (over-reaching pride) and *trais* (oppression), the picture of the Cross between the two thieves whom medieval art depicted so differently, is a spiritual archetype of the greatest importance at the entry into spiritland.

3. Three Streams (Twrch Trwyth)

The tenth battle of Nennius was 'on the shore of the river called Tribruit' ('three streams'), probably transliterated from the Welsh Tryvrwyd ('variegated in colour or surface'). We have indeed reached the farther shore, that of Spiritland. Knowledge of this was shrouded in deep secrecy in the mysteries, and we can expect only tentative hints about it. In considering the Giant (Chapter 3.5) we distinguished the limbs, rhythmic system and head, and the soul processes of willing, feeling and thinking respectively; we are now concerned with the spiritual archetypes of a cosmic order which gave rise to this threefolding. How deeply the idea permeated bardic thinking is shown by the Triads. The aspect of variation can only be taken as referring to the constant mobility and metamorphosis of the archetypes, constantly creating out of themselves anew.

It is necessary first to note that the spiritual world is not just a continuation of the physical, but an inversion of that with which we are normally acquainted, like a glove turned inside out. The wicked hag often turns out to be a beautiful princess, difficulties prove a blessing in disguise, or time sequences are reversed. But it is not always clear which aspect of inversion a given legend adopts.

Time-reversal, for instance, is expressed in the 'Dream of Rhonabwy' in the *Mabinogion*. After a prelude in wretched conditions (ordinary consciousness), Rhonabwy has a dream lasting the usual period of three-and-a-half days, where colours are over-elaborate (Imaginative experience is more saturated than that of daily life). The scene is set after the battle of

Camblan at which Arthur was mortally wounded—Idawg admits his complicity in causing it—so the characters are the living dead, who regard Rhonabwy and his colleagues as 'little men'. Then they go out to fight the battle of Badon, which occurred at least twenty years before Camblan. Again, a young lad, Elphin, reprimands Taliesin's son for splashing Arthur; but Taliesin was only a babe when the adult Elphin found him in a weir. This correctly depicts the reversed experience after death, when we again 'become as little children'.

The next section of *Culhwch*, dealing with the hunt for the Twrch (boar) Trwyth, forms the climax to the tale. This is no ordinary boar, for the story of Torc Truit was also known in Ireland, and *Cormac's Glossary* states that 'a king was called "triath", and "orc triath" is the name for a king's son'. Arthur himself confirms this by saying that 'Twrch Trwyth was a king, whom God changed into a swine for his sins'. And Giant Hawthorn names him as son of Prince Taredd.

The encounter with a wild boar was an Imagination widespread in the mysteries; Osiris, Adonis, Tammuz, the Cretan Zeus and the Irish Diarmuid were each killed by a boar. Arthur is not killed, nor does he aim to kill the boar, only to obtain three 'treasures' and drive it back into the unconscious. Procus/Orcus, the pig, was a symbol for the otherworld in both Greek and Irish mysteries—hence Orcades and Orkneys each doubled as otherworld locations. The sow was specially sacred to Demeter, the earth-mother, and in classical times swine were ritually thrown each autumn into the cave still visible at Eleusis, their remains being recovered to fertilize the seed-corn next spring. The pig-mysteries were thus specifically fertility mysteries—the pig rootles in the earth, using its earthly food in order to absorb cosmic substances from all sides and distribute it throughout its body.[12] As we have already seen (Chapter 3.1), the Arthurian mysteries were pig/boar/sow mysteries.

Looking at the hunt for Twrch Trwyth as the climax of the whole tale, one is struck by the triviality of the objective—the hairdressing of the Giant. What can they be, these three 'treasures between the ears' that must be won? A comb has the ordering, analytical quality of thinking; a razor has the finality of a decision; and shears or scissors play like logic between the two. Together they point to aspects of thought-activity which at that time were a new capacity to be consciously acquired.

We may also be struck by the location of the tale, first in Ireland, then at quite specific places forming a rhythmic path across south Wales, and finally in Cornwall (depicted as extending up the Severn past Bristol). Inverting the hunt so that it pictures the struggle for new capacities, three stages emerge:— The boar-prince rises out of the unconscious into Cornwall and acquires the comb; he follows Arthur to the Severn, where the shears are acquired through Cyledyr (who had been forced by Gwyn to intensify the heart forces) and the razor through Mabon (whose long-frustrated will now had free play). There are nine protagonists in the Severn, including Arthur and Goreu, but two fall fictim to water and rock.

In all the fracas in Wales, none of the marvels specified by the Giant in relation to Twrch Trwyth are mentioned. Sometimes the boar is visible, sometimes the seven piglets, of whom Grugyn Silver-Bristle looks to be a moon-figure and Llwydawg the Demander might represent the earth, so that one is led to think of the sun amid the solar system. In the process of mastering these force-fields with much effort and pain, Grugyn and Llwydawg slay four 'men' including two of Arthur's 'uncles'; two 'men' are slain by the boar at Llwch Ewin, six around Peluniawg, and eight at Cwm Cerwyn, apart from servants, huntsmen and unspecified followers; or rather, through reversal, corresponding faculites are acquired.

Events in Ireland are dominated by Arthur's personal struggle with Trwyth for nine days and nights, the period of Odin's initiation in the Northern mysteries. Arthur is alone more effective than his whole war-band or the forces of Ireland. The boar retires to the Ridge of Cold, and Arthur is blessed by the saints.

The dim outline of three stages of development related to three possible streams of force begins to appear, but the details are hardly susceptible of further comment. Twrch Trwyth is indeed the son of a king—any king—undergoing his training for kingship, thereby becoming a 'boar', a leader inspired by the Arthurian mysteries. He has to acquire and burnish the capacities between the ears; he has to purify his heart forces so as to receive the influences of the planets; and he has to be initiated into the treasures of Hibernia, so that he can grasp the destiny of his people. This is a stage beyond ordinary knighthood, and an indication why Arthur has so many 'kings' in his retinue. The Arthur in charge must himself have mastered the archetypes of these three streams, in order that he can, as hierophant, 'fight alongside' the kings and direct their training correctly. From such a spiritual training alone could the 'divine right of kings' have been derived. A last pale echo of such a process is contained in the coronation ceremony still used today.

4. Agned, Bregion and Badon

It has been thought by scholars[10] that in the Welsh original used by Nennius, the eleventh battle was 'on the hill called Agned' and the twelfth 'on mount Bregion'; that Badon was a scribal substitution for the latter because it was a famous British victory (Gildas mentions 'the siege of Badon hill'); and that Bregion (Breguoin) only survived in the Vatican and Paris manuscripts because it then displaced Agned.

The name 'Agned' is of uncertain meaning, and no conclusions can be drawn from it. In *Culhwch* the final task is to obtain the 'blood of the black witch, daughter of the white witch, from the valley of grief in the uplands of hell'. This again is needed for dressing the Giant's beard. She is found in a cave, which may well represent the entrance to the interior of the earth, where the deepest secrets of evil have their source; but although 'black' she is the daughter of a 'white' witch—evil has its justified place in the divine plan. After she has got the better of two of Arthur's servants and two of his champions,

Arthur himself stood at the entrance to the cave—he could not, as did Christ, descend into hell itself—took aim with his knife, White Hilt, and struck her in the middle 'until she was as two tubs'. Since pictures in spiritland are inverted, this must mean that 'two tubs' were brought together; but what 'two tubs'? We may recall the Chaldean Imagination (Chapter 2.2) of the deed of Marduk/Michael, who at the beginning of the Dark Age ripped consciousness of the demonic Tiamaat into two parts, namely heaven and earth. At this eleventh battle, heaven and earth are reunited: that is to say, the dualism which experiences the sense-world as separate from the spiritual world is finally overcome. This is known to spiritual science as the stage of 'the union between the microcosm and the macrocosm'.

* * * * *

In *Preiddeu Annwn* (Chapter 2.5) the furthest stage was described as 'beyond the glass fort', where there were six-thousand men on the wall with whom it was difficult to communicate. With the twelfth battle on mount Bregion ('heights') or Badon we have not yet reached perhaps the Milky Way, but only the realm of the zodiac. We come in any case to the assertion of Nennius that 'on that one day there fell in one onslaught of Arthur's nine-hundred and sixty men: and none slew them but he alone, and in all his battles he remained victor'. This naturally causes crucial difficulty for those who wish to treat Nennius as a historical source; for it is clearly unscholarly to reject this statement whilst grasping at the rest. As history it is difficult to accept.

But for an interpretation such as the present, this statement simply summarizes the spiritual progress made through the various inner battles we have described, the results of which must all be marshalled 'on one day'. We have referred in passing to various organs of spiritual experience, known by the old Oriental term of 'lotus flowers', which have to be made effective in the astral body, just as there are a number of sense-organs in the physical body. But whereas the physical organs operate naturally in the healthy body, the spiritual organs no longer do so, and must consciously be developed in the right way to become effective. These organs differ in the number of their so-called 'petals', half of which once existed as the basis of atavistic clairvoyance, but have now become inert in nearly all western men; and the other half await unfoldment before the organ can function again in the future. This is done by spiritual exercises which are described in detail by Rudolf Steiner.[11] The first such organ is the two-petal flower between the eyes, developed by logical thought and sound judgement (Chapter 3.2). The twelve-petal flower in the heart region opens perception of the astral world in terms of warmth and cold (Chapter 3.4). The sixteen-petal flower near the larynx gives perception of the world of the elements (Chapter 3.6), and these two should develop together (Chapter 3.7). The ten-petal flower in the pit of the stomach demands control of sense-impressions through a powerful inner life, and opens perception of spiritland (Chaper 4.2). And the eight-petal flower, also in the abdomen, is concerned with forming organs corresponding to planetary influences in the etheric body. Taking the half of each of these that requires development, we arrive at 1 x 8 x 6 x 5 x 4 = 960! Each 'Arthur' had to master each of these 'men' at the same time. It should be added that no claim is made in respect of the six-petal and four-petal flowers, the most demanding. But the factors of 3 and 2 bring the total approximately to 'the six thousand men on the wall' (Chapter 2.5).

We are now in a better position to understand the number of champions slain by Twrch Trwth and his piglets—groups of eight and six, and smaller groups of three, two and one, which may also refer to lotus-flowers. We can also revert to the nine-score 'hoary-headed ones' at the end of the poem *Pa Gur* (Chaper 3.5): this figure includes the developing half of the two, twelve, ten, six and four-petal flowers, but excludes the sixteen-petal flower in the larynx: Cei was notoriously unable to control his bitter tongue and all that flows from it.

The conclusion of *Culhwch* appears barbaric in its ferocity.

Chief Giant Hawthorn, whose power, like Samson, resides in his hair, is shaved to the very bone with the tusk, 'and his two ears outright'. Hair is the outer expression of sun-like rays pouring in from supersensible worlds, and through the ears were received the sounding, shaping forces of the cosmic Word. Culhwch taunts the Giant, and is sharply rebuked that the credit is not his but Arthur's. Culhwch indeed marries Olwen, 'white track', the cosmic higher self. But it is young Goreu who, with the Giant's concurrence, finally cuts off his head and takes possession of all his dominions. Only when this, too, is inverted do we reach the real culmination of this remarkable tale: the redemption of the Giant, representing the whole visible world derived from the Father in which we, and even Arthur, have our origin, by Goreu, the 'best', representing the figure of Jesus Christ within the seeking soul.

5. The Chair-Song of Teyrnon

We may close this section of our enquiry with another poem ascribed to Taliesin, although not composed before the tenth century. The translation has kindly been provided by G. R. Isaac, based on an unpublished study in Welsh by M. Haycock. It differs considerably from the last published version of 1910 by J. Gwenogvryn Evans.

> The recitation of a brilliant poem
> of measureless muse
> about a hero, a brave shaper,
> from the lineage of Aladur.
> Is he a renowned man or a wise man?
> Is he a chieftain of Rheon?
> Is he a lord king?
> With his praise of the scripture
> and his bloody shield
> and his attack over the wall
> and his well-proportioned song.
> Amongst the retinue of the lord
> he took from Cawrnur
> grey saddled horses.

The names in this poem, other than Teyrnon and Arthur, are
unknown elsewhere. The disciplined ego (the lord king) with
its religious and bodily strength leads the well-proportioned
forces of the soul (the retinue of the lord) across the Threshold
of the spiritual world (the wall), bringing back a thinking which
is controlled but shadowy (grey saddled horses). In the tenth
century thinking was normally still felt as something given,
not something controlled by the ego.

> Teyron the elder,
> Heilyn the provider.
> The third abstruse song
> to bless Arthur
> (Arthur is blessed)
> is in harmonious measure.
> A defender in battle,
> one who stamps on nine men.
> Who are the three high officers
> who guarded the country?
> Who are the three poets
> who defended the banner,
> who will come, in accordance with their desire,
> to meet their lord?

Teyron, whose full name means 'Great King of the Raging Sea'
(the inner world), was foster-father to Pryderi, and may be
thought of as representing the divine Father principle. The
third Logos (the abstruse but harmonious song) is the Holy
Spirit, with which Arthur was blessed. The nine men he stamps
out could be the evil daimons corresponding to each of the
Hierarchies, the nine maidens. On crossing the Threshold it
becomes necessary to sacrifice the capacities of ordinary thinking, feeling and willing (the high officers of the ego guarding
the country of daily life) as we saw in the battle with the
threefold Giant (Chapter 3.5). Then the corresponding spiritual
faculties (the three leaders who come as grace and not at man's
bidding) may be received.

> Splendid is the virtue of a ford;
> splendid is weather of lively aspect;

splendid is a horn which carries swiftly;
splendid is the cow by the fresh water;
splendid is wine when it shines:
more splendid, when it speaks
is the drop that came from the cauldron
of the three Ogyrfens.
I have been a lord who wore a torque,
with my horn in my hand.
He does not deserve a chair
who does not preserve my utterance,
a shining song/chair of contest,
an eloquent, certain muse.

Five splendours of the sense-world do not compare with the splendour of inspiration, which is the distinction of the poet entitled to hold the bardic chair.

What is the name of the three fortresses
which are between the tide and the shore?
He who is not zealous does not know
the nature of their mayor.
There are four fortresses
in the lands of Britain.
The lords of the seas' rush
because of what is, it will not be
it will not be because of what is
Fleets are wont to be.
The wave washes over the gravel;
the land of Dylan conquers.
Neither wooded slopes nor a valley
nor a hill nor a hollow
nor a shelter are refuge
from the wind when it rages.
The chair (-song) of Teyrnon,
a skilful man preserves it.

Between the tide and shore is the realm of rhythm, which is experienced in the inspiration already mentioned. The first three fortresses must be the moon and inner planets, whose 'mayor'(?) we described in Chapter 3 as the soul world. The remaining four fortresses were described in Chaper 4 as the spiritland, the sun and outer planets. This is the realm where destiny holds sway, indicated in the fourth and fifth lines above, which are corrupt. Destiny is a spiritual necessity from which there is no refuge—the wind is (as in Hebrew and Greek) the expression of spiritual powers.

> Yngno is sought out,
> Cedig is sought out,
> warriors are lost.
> I deem it a sad way
> to slay the lord;
> in a fiery manner,
> by the armour of legions,
> the lord is exalted.
> Around a shining chieftain
> the vanguard of the army is shattered
> (and/or: the head of the ale is delicate)
> Its nature is broken,
> the tumult on the sea,
> wild around the edge (of the land).
> Foreign peoples
> (are like) the swift flowing
> of the movement of the sea.
> From the children of Seraphin
> (a secret and evil nation)
> let us free Elffin.

The text is so corrupt as to be almost unintelligible, as the variant in the eleventh line shows. But the polarity of 'slaying the lord' and 'the lord is exalted in a fiery manner' seems to hint at the overcoming of the everyday ego and the arising of the higher, eternal ego. In this process the wild tumult of the astral sea is indeed suppressed (broken). We shall revert to the freeing of Elffin/Elphin, representing the higher self, in Chapter 5.4.

But the last verse of another early poem[13] explains Taliesin's chair:

> My chair is preserved in Caer Sidi;
> Disease and old age afflict no one who is there,
> As Manawyt and Pryderi know;
> Havgan's three organs play before it,
> About its peaks are the streams of the ocean,
> And above it is a fruitful fountain;
> Sweeter than white wine is the liquor therein.

Plate 1. The tunnel on the island

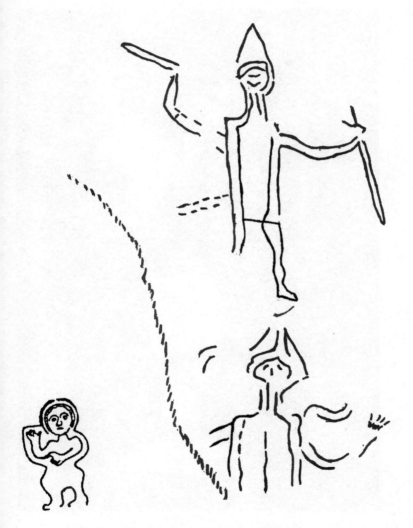

Fig. 1. Human figures from slate and potsherd found at Tintagel, actual size

Plate 3. St. Nectar's Kieve

Plate 4. The left finger-labyrinth, Rocky Valley

Plate 5. The two-petalled lotus flower

Plate 6. The twelve-petalled lotus flower

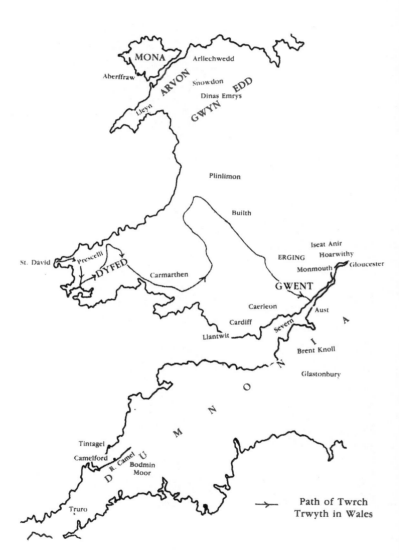

MONA
Arllechwedd
Aberffraw
ARVON
Snowdon
GWYNEDD
Dinas Emrys
Lleyn

Plinlimon

Builth

Iseat Anir
ERGING   Hoarwithy
St. David   Prescelli   Monmouth   Gloucester
DYFED   GWENT
Carmarthen
Caerleon   Aust
Cardiff   Severn
Llantwit   A
N
Brent Knoll

Glastonbury

O

N

M

Tintagel
Camelford   U
R. Camel   Bodmin
D   Moor

Truro

→   Path of Twrch
Trwyth in Wales

'Sidi' is the Welsh equivalent of Irish 'sid', the otherworld, whose root means 'to sit'; Caer Sidi may thus be read as 'the fort of the seat'. 'Havgan' is taken to be a diminutive of 'Avanc', which, as we saw in Chapter 2.2, refers to everyday consciousness, the 'three organs' of which are our thinking, feeling and willing (compare also Chapter 7.4). The chair is thus in the Imaginative world (Chapter 3.6), reaching into the spirit-ocean whose fountain of Inspiration was experienced by Owein (Chapter 3.7).

CHAPTER FIVE

OTHER BRITISH HEROES

1. Owein

The tale of 'The Lady of the Fountain, or Owein' in the *Mabinogion*, has an unusual form, in that the first part of the adventure is related three times. First—and we have already had occasion to consider extracts—it is told as a recollection of Cynon, whilst Arthur sleeps; Cynon is forced to turn back. Owein then goes through the same stages in immediate awareness, and carries the adventure further. Three years later Arthur goes in search of Owein, with Cynon as guide, and beholds all his knights being thrown by Owein, now defending the fountain himself, until Gwalchmei fights him on equal terms for three days, and is finally recognized. As we saw in Chapter 3, 1) The adventure starts in 'the loveliest vale in the world', and 2) leads across a great plain and through a forest 3) to a castle where the hero is welcomed. 4) He is advised to go back and take a different path, where 5) he confronts a huge ugly black man, keeper of the forest, to whom all the animals do obeisance. 6) Although uncivil, the man shows the hero the way to the tree of life and the fountain of wisdom. 7) The hero experiences the hailstorm, the singing birds, and the encounter with the black knight. 8) Trapped by the portcullis of the shining city, he is freed by the love of Luned, the Lady's handmaid, falls in love with the Lady, and through the selfless wooing of Luned on his behalf is enabled to marry the Lady. Arthur arrives and is welcomed to the city with feasting.

It will have been noticed that we have not quoted this tale further, for it now appears to take a 'wrong' turning. Owein receives his Lady's permission to return with Arthur to his court for three months; but he forgets her and overstays, until after three years she sends for her ring back. In remorse he wanders 'the bounds of the earth and desolate mountains', until his clothes perish and he is overcome by weakness. Descending to a valley, he is found by a widowed countess, clothed, and healed by a precious ointment. Owein repays her kindness by capturing the earl who is oppressing her, and forcing him to make redress.

On his way again, Owein frees from a serpent a pure white lion, who thereafter follows him like a hound. While eating they hear groans; it is Luned, imprisoned in a rock for defending his honour because of her love for him. Owein leaves her overnight, and the lion kills the giant who is attacking his host. Then he returns to Luned and fights two youths who come to burn her, and the lion slays them. Luned is now released, and Owein takes his Lady to Arthur's court. As a seeming afterthought, Owein—without the lion—vanquishes the Black Oppressor, who vows to maintain a hospice for weak and strong.

With what is this second part of the story concerned? It seems to tell, in steps less detailed than before, of a different return to Arthur's court from that in *Preiddeu Annwn*, thus completing the circle which began at the gate of birth in battle 1. It is known from classical sources that reincarnation was taught in north-west Europe—for example, Diodorus Siculus quotes Posidonius (c. 90 BC): 'Among them the doctrine of Pythagoras held force, namely that the souls of men are undying, and that after achieving their term of existence they pass into another body.' Caesar said the same of the druids of Gaul. But the return to a new body is not immediate, for the soul must first learn the lessons from its previous life and cast off its remnants, in stages similar to those by which the initiate learns to free himself from his bodies and rise to spiritual experience.

Rudolf Steiner has described[1] how, at the turning point between excarnation and return to a new life, man works for a while on earth, but in the invisible forces, where the consequences of his past deeds are inscribed and must be transformed into future outer destiny. This is expressed in Owein's overlong sojourn back at Arthur's court, the supersensible world adjacent to the sense world. Consciousness then returns to the periphery, the bounds of the world, where all but that moral core which can stand in face of the divine Hierarchies has been cast off, expressed as his remorse; and new impulses are received (long hair grows).

On return to the sun sphere, the court of the Lady finds its counterpart in the castle of the countess (widowed, because Christ has descended from sun to earth). Here Owein receives the healing ointment, which completely transforms the hair into skin even whiter than before (the 'white garments' of the Apocalypse) and corresponds to the receiving of the new astral body (c.f. Gwion in Chapter 3.1). Owein also gains here the strength and courage of the white lion, the new heart forces for the next life. The killing of the serpent points to the overcoming of the Luciferic temptation to remain in spiritual realms as an immature being, which occurs here, and hence the decision to reincarnate.

Owein then comes again upon Luned, whose name points to the moon sphere, although her steadfast love, loyalty and equanimity portray Christ forces reflected from the sun sphere, the court of her mistress. The moon forces carry in extract the destiny of the previous life, and Luned now brings to Owein his destiny with her: as she freed him from the portcullis, so he must now free her from the rock through the strength of the lion. In the moon sphere which focuses the starry forces the etheric body is formed anew.

The final incident with the Black Oppressor marks the return to the physical world, which does indeed oppress the divine forces in man. When defeated, the Black Oppressor vows to become a hospitaller—the physical world will continue to provide bodies for future incarnations, so long as men should have them on the path of involution.

2. Tristan

The story of Tristan and Isolde exists in many different versions, but Gottfried von Strasbourg (fl 1210), author of the most inspired, wrote that 'there have not been many who told this tale aright . . . they did not write according to the authentic version as told by Thomas of Britain (1155/60), who was a master romancer, and had read the lives of all those princes in books of the Britons'.[2] He is aware that Mark, Tristan and Isolde were also historical figures. Only a sixth of the version of Thomas has survived, and there is no reference in it to Arthur, as there is in some others, but Gottfried's reference to Breri (see Chapter 6.1) indicates that its source is the same as that of the Arthurian legends.

The underlying theme is that when the dominion of the intellect becomes an accomplished fact, and religion is no longer understood, the last stronghold of the Divine, in even the humblest human heart, is love.[3] The story is the drama of the soul's development through love, which cannot be commanded, bought or sold, but ultimately only bestowed in perfect freedom. It ranges from demonic desire, through suffering, to the highest deeds of sacrifice—in the urge to go on searching lies the very core of man's being.

Isolde came from Ireland, the home of those who retained the strongest forces of atavistic clairvoyance from Atlantis, together with the corresponding magic arts of healing. In Cornwall were a more advanced group who paid tribute to the horse rather than the bull—the name Mark is in Welsh 'March' (horse)—in whom the intellect came strongly to expression. (The birth of Pryderi points also to a horse cult, though like Tristan himself he later became a 'swineherd'.) Tristan himself comes from Parmenie, whose whereabouts are left unclear: the name derives from Para-manas, the soul land. He is, according to the Triads, son of Tallwch, (the one who thrusts down', the lust of the astral body) and one of the Three Battle-Coroneted men of Britain. His guardian is Rual the faith-keeper. The love of his father Rivalin for Mark's sister Blanche-flur is purely physical, hence he is depicted as wounded by a spear.

Tristan is protrayed as being far beyond his contemporaries in every kind of ability. Kidnapped by merchants, but released in fear of divine retribution, he reaches Mark's court and wins his affection. In Cornwall he adds to his gifts that of the intellect, and begins to place it in the service of the spirit. When Morold comes from Ireland to collect tribute of young men and women, Tristan resists—Gottfried says that on his side were God, Right, Courage and Tristan himself, namely his spiritual attributes—and he kills Morold, a fragment of his sword remaining in Morold's skull. But Morold's sword was poisoned with lower astrality, Tristan succumbs to a loathsome disease. He travels to Ireland disguised as Tantris, through his singing and lute-playing ingratiates himself with the Queen, and is healed by her magic arts. In exchange he instructs Isolde, her daughter, in music. On his return to Mark's court he praises her so much that Mark would have her, and Tristan undertakes to woo her on his behalf.

Having destroyed a dragon marauding Ireland he is under the Queen's protection when Isolde identifies him as Tristan through the gap in his sword. She raises the sword to kill him, but lets it fall: past karma intervenes—the hate which filled her is unrecognized love. The Queen makes a potion intended to augment the bodily union of Isolde and Mark by a union of soul through recognition of their karma in previous lives; but by 'chance' it is Tristan and Isolde who drink it. What bound them in past lives overwhelms their minds. Tristan undergoes suffering on account of earthly love, something unknown in Parmenie from whence he came. He lies to and deceives his friend Mark. When Brangane gives herself up to Mark in place of Isolde, she represents the fully-awake earthly nature of Isolde, whose soul never belongs to him. Through guilt and pain, Tristan learns to distinguish between the things of God and those of Caesar. There are two courtiers, described as the dog (earthly consciousness) and the serpent (desire) who continually warn Mark. Tristan tries to rescue Isolde and himself from sensuality under the olive tree (symbol of anointment with the oil of wisdom); but the shadow of their guilt confronts them in the shape of Mark and the serpent. It is from the magic of the past that Isolde knows how to hold the red-hot iron without being burned. Their life oscillates between their rights as lovers and their outward guilt. In Wales Tristan kills a 'giant', and receives a fairy dog of seven colours (sevenfold divine wisdom) wearing a little bell which drives away all sorrows, the peace of self-understanding. Isolde receives the dog, but tears off the bell—she does not wish to be at peace, and continually drags Tristan down. Mark's jealousy banishes the lovers from court, but he still hankers after Isolde. Tristan flees Mark's country, and labours to love Isolde of the White Hands, but cannot put the first Isolde from his mind—the two are the two aspects of love itself, sensual and spiritual. He dies of sorrow: Isolde's old clairvoyance is indeed black, like the black sail, it is unpurified astrality.

The Welsh fragments do not add significantly to this saga; but there is an interesting conversation[4]: 'after Trystan had been absent three years from Arthur's court in displeasure, and Arthur had sent eight-and-twenty warriors to seize him, and bring him to Arthur, Trystan smote them all down, one after another, and came not for any one, but for Gwalchmei of the Golden Tongue.' After seven exchanges in triplets of mutual respect Trystan says: 'Gwalchmei, for thy sake will I deliberate, And with my mouth I utter it—As I am loved, so will I love.'

3. Merlin

The Welsh name 'Myrddin' means 'sea-dweller', and can be
regularly derived from Moridunon (Carmarthen); but it is likely
to be older. According to a suspect Triad 'The first name that
this island bore, before it was taken or settled: Myrddin's
precinct'. Geoffrey of Monmouth's statement in his *History*[5]
that Merlin by his magic moved stones from 'Mount Killarus
in Ireland' to Stonehenge and set them up there—in what is
now recognized as an astronomical orientation—echoes his
real part in carrying something of the star lore of the Hibernian
mysteries into the mysteries of Britain at the end of the
megalithic period. Rudolf Steiner spoke of Merlin as a priest
of the Hibernian mysteries whose teaching was fostered at
Tintagel. And Geoffrey's description of the 'birth of Arthur'
as a result of Merlin's power of shape-shifting, then falls into
place as the founding of the Arthurian mystery school.

The elusive quality of Myrddin in Welsh tradition was sum-
marized by Elis Gruffyd about 1520 as follows:[6] 'Some hold
the opinion and firmly say that Myrddin was a spirit in man's
form, who continued in that state from the time of Vortigern
until the beginning of Arthur, when he disappeared. And after
this, the spirit appeared a second time in the time of Maelgwyn
Gwynedd (died c.560), at which time he is called Taliesin, who
is said to be still alive in a city called Caer Sidia (i.e., the otherworld). Thence he appeared the third time in the time of Morfryn the Freckled, son of Essyllt (fl 826), whose son he was
said to be, and this time was called Myrddin the Wild. And
from that day to this it is said he rests in Caer Sidia, whence
certain people believe without a doubt that he will arise once
again before the day of Judgement.' Triad 87 names the 'Three
Skilful bards' at Arthur's court as Myrddin son of Morfryn,
Myrddin Emrys and Taliesin.

We considered in Chapter 3.1 Geoffrey's story of the birth
of Merlin Ambrosius (Emrys)—called by Nennius Ambrosius,

not Merlin—as the son of 'a spirit that partakes of the nature of both men and angels'. The boy, discovered at Carmarthen, predicted to Vortigern that his tower's repeated collapse would be found due to its being built on a pool; beneath this pool were two stone slabs, under which two dragons were fighting; and that although at first the white one had the upper hand, the red would eventually conquer. This Geoffrey explains as the conflict between Saxon and British, and as such the prediction has failed. But such pictures may have several meanings— for example, that intelligence was descending from the etheric to the physical brain (pool and stone slabs), and that the ruling moon-initiation (white) would give way to a new sun-initiation (red).

A quite separate ancient and widespread story, current in Scotland and Ireland, told of a bard Lailoken driven out of his mind by a vision during a battle that he had partly occasioned, who fled to the forest, lived wild, and was endowed with prophecy. At length he met a saint who recorded his predictions and absolved him. But having disclosed to the king the adultery of his queen, he is at her instigation stoned by shepherds, falls into the Tweed and is impaled on a stake, and drowns—thus dying a 'mystical threefold death'. Although the name Myrddin is not in any northern source, and such a death is not in any Welsh source, Lailoken became identified with 'Myrddin the Wild'. In the *Cyfoesi* (tenth century) his sister speaks of 'my Llalogen Myrddin'. Myrddin however here asserts: 'I will not take communion from loathsome monks, with their pouches on their thighs; may God himself communicate me.' In his *Vita Merlini*[7] Geoffrey develops the story. He adds a dramatic incident where Merlin rides out of the forest on a stag to the wedding of the wife he had deserted. Seeing the bridegroom laugh, he tears off the stag's antlers, hurls them at him, and kills him—the ancient stag forces of Cerunnos (Chapter 2.2) are obsolete and turn to evil.

Another, separate northern saga of the battle of Arfderydd near Carlisle in 573 told how king Gwenddolau ('of the luminous oblique courses', one of the 'three Bull-Protectors' of Triad 6) was slain. Since, most unusually, the defenders showed rare self-reliance by continuing 'for a fortnight and a month after their lord was slain' (Triad 29), it must have been a centre of vital importance to the bull-cult (Chapter 2.2), suppressed by the Christian king Rhydderch. N. Tolstoi has shown[8] how a Myrddin who was prophet to Gwenddolau lost his reason and fled to Hart Fell in the Caledonian forest, living by a spring below an eminence called 'Arthur's seat'. Here an historical situation merges with the legendary sources, giving rise to the Myrddin 'in the time of Maelgwyn Gwynedd'.

But the passage from the *Vita Merlini* which describes Merlin as working at an observatory in 'Celidon wood' with seventy doors and seventy windows, opening the books of inspiration and making his prophecies (Chapter 3.7), clearly speaks not of a 'wild man' but of an initiate. We hear of him meditating on 'the red Mars and the double ray of Venus'. His reputation as a real person is manifest in the *Armes Prydain* written in Dyved about 930, which says repeatedly 'Merlin foretells. . . .' Although the prophecies incorporated by Geoffrey in his *History* were probably written in the eleventh-twelfth centuries, they came to be considered of sufficient importance for Alanus ab Insulis of Chartres to write a commentary on them. They should not therefore be dismissed too superficially.

Stewart has shown[9] that the prophecies fall into three groups: those relating to events interpreted as reaching from the sixth century to today; mythical images such as the triad of life, desire and death, or the relationship of sovereignty to land, and a dozen animal parables; and some apocalyptic visions. Let us consider briefly the latter, with mere hints of a possible interpretation. They begin with the words 'Root and branch shall change places, and the newness of the thing shall pass as a miracle.' Just such a change from a material (root) science to a branch (spiritual) science is now taking place. We hear of 'the Sun fading at Mercury'—the Sun Being descending to mankind as Healer—and 'Mars calling Venus'—the impulse of self-assertion seeking balance through love. A remarkable paragraph follows: 'The Gemini shall omit their usual embrace, and will call Aquarius to the fountains.' The two forces of evil described in Chapter 4.2, hitherto regarded as unity—Lucifer who tempts to egoism and Ahriman who drags man down into matter—must now be distinguished; and in the coming age when the vernal point is in Aquarius men must learn to hold the balance between them as etheric forces (fountains). Next, 'The scales of Libra shall hang awry till Aries puts his crooked horns under them.' Such balance is only possible through the help of the Lamb with the crook, as Christ was depicted in medieval times. Then comes 'The tail of Scorpio shall produce lightning, and Cancer quarrel with the Sun.' This points to the cataclysm in the following age described in the 'Little Apocalypse' (Mark xiii), which leads in the Apocalypse from the Letters to the Seals. Scorpio brings death to all that is old, Cancer always marks a new beginning from the old. And now 'Virgo shall mount on the back of Sagittarius and darken her virgin flowers.' In the first age of the Seals (the horseman with the bow) the present method of reproduction (the virgin flowers) will no longer be effective. Rudolf Steiner has described[10] how, in some 6000 years' time, mankind will no longer be able to master the bodies already showing signs of ageing, and will through the larynx create bodies of a more cloudlike nature (this is connected with Christ's second coming 'in the clouds'). At this apocalyptic time 'The chariot of the Moon shall disturb the Zodiac'—the moon will reunite with the earth—'and the Pleiades break forth into weeping'—rising and setting of the Pleiades marked the festivals of Beltane and Samhain distinguishing summer from winter, hence the seasons will be disturbed by the moon which dominates the fluid-element (weeping).

'None of these shall return to his wonted duty. Ariadne will shut its door and be hidden within the enclosing clouds.' Ariadne/Arianrhod were forms of the Guardian of the Threshold (Chapter 3.3). The new mankind will be of etheric nature and cease to incarnate physically (the shutting of the door), but take form in the clouds. Finally, 'The seas shall rise up in the twinkling of an eye, and the dust of the ancients be restored; the winds shall fight together with a frightful blast, and their sound shall reach the stars.' In the further process of involution the elements of earth, water and air will be dissolved, but the sound will work on into the future ('My Word shall not pass away'). This may give some feeling for another aspect of Merlin's star lore.

It will have been noticed that Gruffyd said that Myrddin Ambrosius continued 'until the beginning of Arthur, when he disappeared'. There is no mention in either Welsh tradition or in Geoffrey of his continuing to guide Arthur and his knights. The picture which degrades Myrddin to a kind of super-magician comes from the prose *Merlin* (about 1200) ascribed to Robert de Boron, who was an advocate of the Grail stream (Chapter 6.4) as distinct from the Arthurian. This first records the kingship test of Arthur drawing the sword from the stone, drawing thoughts from the mineral kingdom through his own strength, rather than receiving them clairvoyantly as hitherto. It also contains the stories of Merlin instituting the Round Table—appropriately—but adds the Siege Perilous and magic writing; the warning to Arthur of the tragic consequences of marrying Guinevere (turning back to moon-wisdom); and similar themes of Merlin's intervention. It also speaks of Merlins attachment to Viviane, one of the nine 'Ladies of the Lake', to whom he taught his magic arts that she might at least in part succeed him. He allowed her to immure him in a tower without walls or chains, by ninefold enchantment alone (Malory: under a great stone in Cornwall) 'that you may sleep through many centuries till the day dawns for you to awake'. This may be a remnant of belief in reincarnation, or the connecting of Merlin as prophet with the coming again of 'Arthur'.

Welsh tradition tells how Myrddin the Wild finally withdrew to Bardsey, the sacred island of the dead off the Lleyn peninsula, with nine attendant bards, and took with him the 'Thirteen Treasures of the Island of Britain'. Here his abode was a house of glass, a whitethorn in bloom, or 'an inclosure neither of iron, steel, wood nor stone but of air, without any other thing, by enchantment so strong that it may never be undone'. This must have been in 'Caer Sidia'. He predicted of himself: 'My flesh will be corrupt, but my spirit will never cease to speak with those who seek me.'

Taken together, we thus have a picture of a superhuman Being indwelling various individuals, with the particular ability to read the inspirations of the stars. Bearing in mind the early connection with Chaldea (Chapter 2.2) and the similarity of names (Chapter 1.3) we may observe the similarity between the name Myrddin and Chaldean Merodach/Marduk, the Hebrew Michael; but any connection can certainly not be asserted. Speaking, however, immediately after his visit to Tintagel, Rudolf Steiner described in detail[12] how 'the whole configuration of this castle at Tintagel indicates that the twelve under the direction of King Arthur were essentially a Michael-community, belonging to the age when Michael administered still the Cosmic Intelligence. This was actually the community which worked longer than any other to ensure that Michael should retain his dominion over the Cosmic Intelligence.' And, as said above, it was Merlin's teaching which was fostered at Tintagel.

4. Taliesin

Only about a dozen of the fifty-seven poems anciently ascribed to Taliesin are thought to be actually the work of a poet of that name writing between 550 and 590, and they are all panegyrics to historical rulers, notably Urien Rheged, to whom he was court poet. The remainder were written some time between the tenth and twelfth centuries, and ascribed to him on account of his reputation. We have already quoted the two of these most relevant to our subject (Chapters 2.5 and 4.5) and referred to others (Chapter 3.6).

We may now consider the tale known as 'The Story of Taliesin', which exists in various different versions, none of them earlier than the sixteenth century, although the poems inserted in them may well date back to the tenth. We follow that published last century by Lady Guest,[4] which is somewhat more detailed. Merry[13] has said of this that the events in their sequence 'represent the true order of initiation experiences: first there has been the passage through the elemental world and the memory of pre-natal existence; then the loss of the earthly personality (or lower self) who is in prison and, in a sense, suffers because of humanity; and then, when face to face with the loss (which is a loss on both sides) the whole reality of the spiritual nature of the human being is recognized and the path of evolution is seen "from the beginning". And then something of the law of destiny reveals itself.'

This tale is set 'in the beginning of Arthur's time', largely at the court of Maelgwyn Gwynedd, who actually ruled some forty years after the 'historical' Arthur. It begins with the relatively independent story of Ceridwen's cauldron and the adventures of little Gwion, which was quoted in Chapter 3.1 as an example of pre-earthly experience in the astral and etheric worlds. After passing through Ceridwen's womb, Gwion is cast adrift on the sea and found in a weir by Elphin. He is then named Taliesin, 'radiant brow', implying that the two-petal lotus flower is already active. The babe is immediately inspired with wisdom from above, and speaks 'The Consolation of Elphin' (who was disappointed not to have found a bag of gold). This contains the injunctions: 'Doubt not the miracles of the Almighty . . . Be not displeased at thy misfortune . . . Thou has not much to fear . . .' This can remind us of the overcoming of the three Giants of ordinary thinking, feeling and willing (Chapter 3.5). Asked what he was, the babe's reply was translated by Davies as follows:[11]

I was first modelled in the form of a pure Man in the hall of
Ceridwen.
Though small within my chest and modest in deportment, I
was (then) great.
A sanctuary carried me above the surface of the earth;
Whilst I was enclosed within its ribs, the sweet muse rendered
me complete.
And my law was imparted to me without audible language
By the old giantess, darkly smiling in her wrath.

Again we have the principle steps of incarnation: the forming
of the great spirit-germ in the cosmos, the completing of the
astral body by the 'sweet muse', and the incorporation of the
karmic extract from the previous life ('my law') into the etheric
body prior to physical birth. The poem goes on to list the sixteen metamorphoses, given in Chapter 3.6, and the casting
adrift. To Elphin's father he sang:

In water there is a quality endowed with a blessing;
On God it is most just to meditate aright . . .
Three times have I been born, I know by meditation;
It were miserable for a person not to come and obtain
All the sciences of the world collected together in my breast,
For I know what has been, what in future will occur . . .

When Taliesin is thirteen, Elphin gets into trouble with the king
and is imprisoned, and Taliesin goes to release him. After he
has reduced the court bards to playing 'blerwm' on their lips,
he replies to the king's question

My original country is the region of the summer stars;
Idno and Heinin called me Merddin, at length every king will
call me Taliesin.
I was with my Lord in the highest sphere
On the fall of Lucifer into the depth of hell . . .
I know the names of the stars from north to south,
I have been on the galaxy at the throne of the Distributor . . .
I have been loquacious before being gifted with speech . . .
I am a wonder whose origin is not known . . .
I have been with my Lord in the manger of the ass . . .
I have been teacher to all Intelligences . . .
I shall be until the day of doom on the face of the earth;
And it is not known whether my body is flesh or fish.

This can only be understood as the expression of a soul entirely united with the Spirit of Mankind and thereby with Christ, an experience of the higher self. If lines in the next poem appear as the boasting of Lucifer—'Three-hundred songs and more are combined in the spell I sing'—this is balanced by a fine picture of Ahriman in that which follows:

There is a noxious creature
From the ramparts of Satanas
Which has overcome all
Between the deep and the shallow;
Equally wide are his jaws
As the mountains of the Alps;
Him death will not subdue
Nor hand or blades. . .
There is in his head an eye
Green as the limpid sheet of icicle. . .

After several poems challenging the bards, Taliesin intones a long riddle which calls up a mighty storm of wind. Elphin is brought from the dungeon, and Taliesin's next poem, 'I adore the Supreme, Lord of all animation. . .' opens his chains. After further poems on bardism and the miraculous discovery of a bag of gold, the tale ends with a poem describing the creation of man, in biblical terms.

* * * * *

We may turn next to the poem referred to in Chapter 3.6, scrambled to withhold Bardic secrets, from which Robert Graves[14] has extracted three meaningful units: 'the battle of the trees', dealing with the conflict of Bran and Beli and the creation of the bardic alphabet; the creation of the flower-maiden Blodeuwedd; and of the corresponding fruit-man. From the residue we quoted in Chapter 3.6, lines referring to the elements of earth, water, air and fire; we can add to this the etheric formative forces of light, sound and life:

I have been a light in a lantern
A year and a half
I have been the string of a harp
I have been the string of a child's swaddling clout.

Further lines reach out not only to the movements of the planets, but also to previous conditions of the earth itself:

I know the star-knowledge
Of stars before earth was,
How many worlds there are
Whence I was born.
I have been a dark star formerly.
I have been a shining star.
I know the light whose name in Splendour,
And the number of ruling lights
That scatter rays of fire
High above the deep.

We may end by quoting some lines from 'The Great Song of the World':[15]

I will praise my Father
My God, my strength,
Who has given me in my head
Soul and reason,
And has made for my advantage
My seven senses,
And fire and earth, and water and air,
And clouds and flowers
And wind and trees . . .
Seven firmaments there are
High above the stars
And three divisions of the sea.
The sea is beating on all sides;
The sea is very wonderful;
It entirely surrounds the earth.
God made the (firmament) above
For the planets . . .

This may give some impression of the understanding surviving from the mysteries in Wales.

CHAPTER SIX

AFTER TINTAGEL

1. The Move to Wales

We cannot be sure when the Arthurian mysteries left Tintagel, but there are clues. The Cornish sources used by Geoffrey of Monmouth seem to have believed that the Arthur killed by Mordred was returning to base behind the river Camel, which implies that they thought of Tintagel as his centre up to his death, in 539 according to the *Annales Cambriae*. On the other hand it would be reasonable to suppose that the move took place before the threat of the Saxons to overrun Cornwall became critical, although this was in fact averted by the battle of Badon, the date of which may be either 490 or 518 (and Arthur was probably not involved).

St Sampson is said[1] to have passed through Cornwall on his way from Wales to Brittany some time after 520—he attended the Council of Paris in 560. 'Now as he passed through a district called Tricuria, he heard that in the northern part men were worshipping at a certain temple after the manner of Bacchantes through a dramatic representation (*imaginariam ludum*).' Trigg was a petty kingdom whose capital was at Helston, south of Camelford, and Tintagel lay towards its northern end. We may also recall that Cyprian of Antioch experienced at Tempe, which was in close contact with Britain, 'dramatic performances of demons in conflict' (Chapter 2.4). Sampson hastened to them (taking two brethren) and greatly remonstrated with them for forsaking the one God who made all things, to worship an idol. All this while their chieftain Geudianus was standing before them. They began to excuse themselves by saying there was no harm in observing the magical rites of their ancestors in a play. Some were angry, some scoffed, while the more polite among them urged him to go away. But suddenly the power of God was openly displayed when a certain boy engaged in horse-racing was thrown to the ground from a swift horse, and twisting his neck as he fell headlong, lay like a corpse.' St Sampson of course 'restored the youth to life', in return for which Guedianus and his followers agreed to be baptised.

If this does refer to Tintagel, which is uncertain, the mention of 'magical rites of their ancestors' suggests that the centre had ceased to be active a least a generation earlier, and would confirm a date of departure in the fifth century. Rudolf Steiner mentions in passing, the activity of the mystery centre there 'during the first four centuries'. The major phase of construction already excavated is assigned to the sixth century, when the vacant site may well have been adapted to a new use, which impending excavations may determine.

To where, then, did the Arthurian mystery centre move? Triad 1 says that Arthur had three 'tribal thrones', at Celliwig in Cornwall, Pen Rhionedd in the North (location uncertain, possibly the tip of Galloway), and St Davids in Wales—but this is now regarded[2] as substituted by a scribe there, for Aberffraw on the south coast of Anglesey. Since the North was also under threat it is most likely that the centre moved to Wales, where the oldest manuscripts relating to Arthur are found. But the name of Arthur is so widely spread across the map of Britain that it would be unwise to assume that the 'tribal thrones' were the only centres.

Bearing in mind the practice of bards to hide their more intimate information in symbolism, there is another extremely curious Triad which may perhaps be relevant. We have seen evidence of a stag cult, a bull cult (Chapter 2.2) and a horse

cult. We should not, therefore, be surprised to find the
Arthurian mysteries, which we have already seen to be
connected with the pig or boar, referred to as a prolific sow.
Triad 26 includes the following story, the longest in the Triads:
'Coll, son of Collfrewy, guarded the swine of Dallwyr
Dallben in the valley of Dallwyr in Cornwall. And one of the
swine was pregnant, Henwen (old white) was her name. And
it was prophesised that the Island of Britain would be the worse
for the womb-burden. Then Arthur assembled the host of the
Island of Britain, and set out to seek to destroy her. And then
she set off, about to bring forth, and at Penrhyn Awstin in
Cornwall (Aust point near Bristol?) she entered the sea, the
powerful swineherd after her. And at Aber Tarogi in Gwent
Iscoed (just opposite) she came to land; and Coll son of
Collfrewy with his hand on her bristles wherever she went,
whether by sea or by land. And in the Wheatfield in Gwent
she brought forth a grain of wheat and a bee; and therefore
from that day to this the Wheatfield in Gwent is the best place
for wheat and bees. And from there she went to Lonio in Pembroke, and there she brought forth a grain of barley and a bee
(var: grain of wheat); and therefore the best barley is in Dyved.
At the Hill of Effort in Arvon she brought forth a wolf-cub and
a young eagle; and Coll son of Collfrewy gave the eagle to
Breat, a prince of the North (var. Brennach the Irishman) and
the wolf he gave to Menwaedd of Arllechwedd; and they were
both the worse for them. And from there she went to the Black
Rock in Llanfair in Arvon, and there she brought forth a kitten;
and Coll son of Collfrewy threw that kitten from the rock into
the Menai. And the sons of Palug fostered it in Mon (Anglesey),
to their own harm; and that was afterwards Palug's Cat, and
it was one of the Three Great Oppressions of Anglesey nur-
tured therein.'

This strange tale is thought likely to have been composed
as early as the sixth century—not long after the move from
Tintagel—although first written down in the 11th century.
Coll, 'hazel', is the tree of wisdom, poetry, white magic and

healing;[3] and he is one of the Three Great Enchanters of Britain. Dallwyr Dallben, 'blind man/mystic, blindhead', comes from the valley of mystics in Cornwall—one thinks of Rocky Valley. If Wheatfield in Gwent is taken as reaching up the Wye valley, we come to an important area that will be described further in relation to the Celtic church (Chapter 6.2) and to the Welsh legends of Arthur (Chapter 6.3), perhaps the staff of life and the honey of esotericism, respectively.

Dyved was the home of Pryderi son of Pwyll ('deep thought', son of 'meaning'), the key character of the Four Branches of the *Mabinogion*, who had a special relationship to the mysterious realm of Annwm, the 'in-world'. We touch here the mysteries of Ceridwen, reputedly like Demeter a barley-goddess, and the centre at Presceli from where the bluestones were removed to Stonehenge.

The Hill of Effort in Arvon, which sounds like a centre of spiritual striving, has been identified with Snowdon; and Beroul, in his *Tristan*, depicted Iseult's squire seeking Arthur first at Tintagel, and eventually finding him seated at the Round Table in Isneldoune (Snowdon). Breat is not otherwise known, but Brennach was a fifth-sixth century saint who made the pilgrimage to Rome, and was thus associated with the eagle.

To Arllechwedd, the magic swine from Annwn, guarded by Pryderi and stolen by Gwydion, were taken in the story of 'Math' in the *Mabinogion*. There, on the north flank of Snowdon, lie the stone circles of Penmaenmawr, once a centre of the Northern mysteries, which were also active in Britain and are well represented by the wolf-cub. Gwydion has indeed been identified with Odin/Wotan.[3] In the consequent battle Gwydion killed Pryderi by magic, and in punishment he and his brother were turned by Math into animals, and gave birth successively to a fawn, a piglet and a wolf-cub. Restored to human shape, it was a sow which at length led Gwydion to recover his son Lleu Llaw Gyffes (found hanging from a tree wounded by a spear, as was Wotan), in the form of an eagle. We thus find a sequence of animals in this tale similar to those in the Triad of Henwen. Through Gwydion we make contact with Beli (Chapter 2.4) and the House of Don, and the Tuatha de Danaan in Ireland.

The kitten that became the Palug Cat—whose 'scratch' reduced Cei's shield to a fragment (Chapter 3.5)—can only represent the final decline of the Round Table, incorporating the last decadent remnants of the druid culture exterminated by the Romans in 61 AD, and fighting like a wild cat for survival when all its spirituality had been lost.

2. Origins of the Welsh Church

We saw in Chapter 4.2 that the descent of Christ from the sun to the earth was foreseen in the Arthurian mysteries. And when, through the flowing of the blood of Christ on the Cross, the Sun Spirit became the Spirit of the Earth ('I will remain with you unto the end of the earth'), the whole relationship between the elemental beings born of the sunlight and those rising in the seething spray changed so radically, that the twelve around Arthur could read the fact that the Mystery of Golgotha had indeed taken place. Britain thus became permeated from the beginning by Christianity.

We have no written proof of this until Tertullian wrote about 203 of 'places in Britain which, though inaccessible to the Romans, had yielded to Christ'. And according to Bede 'the Britons received the faith and held it peacefully in all its purity and fullness until the time of the emperor Diocletian' (303). In 314 there were already three British bishops at the council of Arles. There were consequently no martyrs in the early Celtic church—'merthyr' originally meant 'shrine', and only later became connected with martyrdom.

According to a remark of Rudolf Steiner,[4] the teachings of Dionysius the Areopagite were received with great understanding in the mysteries of Wales and Britain. He was leader of the esoteric school of St Paul in Athens, from which the esoteric stream of Christian wisdom flowed, independently of the Roman hierarchy, guided as to method by St John's Gospel, and as to content by the Apocalypse. Dionysius left a clear synthesis of etheric star lore and Christianity, which was very much in harmony with the Arthurian mystery tradition. He taught that in Christ the sun forces formed a new connection between the earth and the divine Hierarchies, so that those cosmic powers that bring forth vegetation were concentrated in the bread before it became flesh, and those that form the essence of man were present in the wine before it became blood. The Eucharist was understood in the Celtic church in this sense. The teaching handed down from Dionysius was known to have been tampered with before it was published in the sixth century as the work of the so-called 'pseudo-Dionysius'.

Steiner also described something else which sheds much light on this situation.[5] The unity of each of the different peoples on earth is not a chance affair, but the result of the working of a particular Archangel as Folk Spirit. It was because the Folk Spirit of the Celtic people renounced his task in order to become the leader of this stream of esoteric Christianity that the Celts lost their cohesion as a united people about this time. It was, however, they who were later able to become bearers of the esoteric Christianity connected with the Grail.

The Celtic church (details of which come mainly from Ireland) spoke of 'attending the mysteries' and of 'the communion of the mysteries', evidently conscious of the origin of the Mass. It was Trinitarian, like the bardic tradition. The Father was felt both in the primal energies of the earth, and in the inherited blood stock. But creation of all the objects of the visible world was ascribed to the Logos or Word, the Son, in accordance with the opening of St John's Gospel. Christ is ruler of the earth, and each individual must find Him here in spirit, in consciousness, for He had Himself given man his individuality. Thus no priest, saint or angel was needed as mediator between man and Christ, there was no concept of

earthly hierarchy. Services were consequently in the ver-
nacular, for instruction rather than mediation; and there was
no interest in dogma, such as that of the Virgin Birth, or in
the decrees of church councils, but only in individual work
with the gospels.[6]

In 397 Ninian, with the support of twelve disciples, founded
the abbey of Whithorn (known as 'Candida Casa') on the tip
of Galloway (see Chapter 6.1); and this pattern of twelve sup-
porters was widely followed. Meanwhile, between 394 and
418 Pelagius was preaching in Rome the Celtic Christianity of
Ireland, and it is very likely that he would have visited Tintagel
on his way there. He asserted direct communion between the
individual Christian and Christ without priestly mediation, but
with trust instead in the Johannine assertion 'You shall know
the truth, and the truth shall set you free.'[7] This of course
undermined the authority of the Roman hierarchy, and this
was the real cause of the strong opposition from Rome to the
Celtic church. (Differences in the date of celebrating Easter
were minimal; they arose only when the day of full moon was
itself a Sunday, and were due to the fact that Rome changed
the rule after 455, and the Celtic church saw no reason to
depart from the traditional date—again a question of
authoritarianism.) Pelagius was anathematized and banished,
and determined efforts were made to suppress his views in
Britain in the anti-Pelagian persecution by Germanus in 429
and 440. But it was purported heresy, not paganism, that he
attacked. He did not however touch Cornwall or Wales, where
Celtic Christianity was strong and had the support of the
Arthurian mysteries. All sources are unanimous that Arthur
'held court' at the Christian festivals of Christmas, Easter and
Whitsun, and not at the old Celtic festivals of Samain, Beltane
or Lammas. It is only in the later 'lives of the saints' deriving
from the Roman church that he is depicted as an opponent
or tyrant.

The fifth century was an age of great expansion of Celtic
Christianity, particularly in Cornwall, where the map is still

covered with the names of saints who settled at the head of a valley, or on a spur. The churchyard of St Materiana in Tintagel with its oval shape (before extension) is typical of such an enclosure, and although it cannot be dated, it is possible that it co-existed with the Arthurian centre before that departed from the promontory. There can have been no dispute that it was to become the task of the church to carry Christianity to the people, and that those tending the inner mysteries should withdraw.

An interesting illustration of this comes from the petty kingdom of Erging, between Wye and Usk, Monmouth and Hereford, which may be the 'Wheatfied' of the Henwen tale. It was the home of the Silures, the only Welsh tribe to have resisted the Roman army tenaciously; and their king Lucius was said nevertheless to have sought baptism in Rome very early (c. 175). The first monastery in the south had been founded at Llantwit (west of Cardiff) in 523 by Illtuyd, said to be a 'soldier' or 'cousin' of Arthur, who 'taught a new method of ploughing' (the root 'Art-' means to plough—Chapter 8.3). Among his students were David, Sampson, Gildas, and Dyfrig, founding father of the Welsh church (latinized as Dubricius, whom Geoffrey casts as archbishop to Arthur and who, according to the Book of Llandaff, crowned him in 506 AD). Dyfrig was a grandson of king Peibio of Erging, who in a celebrated argument had claimed the stars as his flock and the moon as his shepherd. Dyfrig founded his own monastery at Hentland, some 5m. N of Ross-on-Wye, moved a couple of miles north as the Saxons approached to a more defensible position at Llanfrother, 'church of the brothers', near Hoarwithy. According to the book of Llandaff he 'retained 2000 clergy for seven successive years at Hentland, in the literary study of divine and human wisdom'. Whence did he assemble them? It continues: 'At another time he stayed with his disciples on the island of Eurrdil (his mother's name), giving it the name Mochros ("swine moor", modern Moccas). And rightly was it so called, for during the preceding night an Angel of the Lord appeared to him in a dream and said, "See that on the morrow thou go all around the place which thou hast proposed, and when thou wilt see a white sow lying with her pigs, there lay a foundation.". As the Angel had promised him, a white sow with her piglets got up before them, and there he constructed an oratory and an habitation.'

Is this connection with the sow Henwen (old white) mere coincidence? Is it coincidence that St Brynach founded his church on the river Nevern in Pembroke after a similar angelic guidance, at the point where he saw 'a white sow with white piglets'; that St Cadog, similarly guided, founded his where he saw 'a singular big boar rise up, and a swan of white colour flying away'; that Tyfai, a disciple of Dyfrig, died in Pembrokeshire in defence of a swineherd; and that even St Patrick was a swineherd in his youth?

We can now reconsider the story of Nennius mentioned in Chapter 2.6: 'In Erging there is a burial mound near a spring known as the Eye of Anir/Amr (the source of the Gamber near Wormelow, where there was a tumulus before the main road was altered). And the name of the man buried in the mound is Anir. He was the son of Arthur the soldier, and Arthur killed him there and buried him. And men come to measure the length of the mound, and they find it sometimes 6ft, sometimes 9ft, sometimes 12ft, sometimes 15ft. Whatever length you find it at one time, you will find it different at another, and I myself have proved this to be true.'

The last provocative remark shows that Nennius wrote metaphorically. Moreover, Arthur's son is called Lacheu ('glitterer', Loholt in the Romances) except for a single remark in *Gereint* which may derive from this very passage. We may recall that in *Preiddeu Annwn* (Chapter 2.5) the clergy who 'throng together like wolves', instead of taking the individual path of the mysteries, were described as cowards ('annwr'). Moreover 6ft to 15ft are typical sizes for the small oratories of the time, where services were conducted standing. The one at Tintagel was 9ft (Chapter 1.1).

We can hardly escape the conclusion that various Arthurian foundations (not necessarily 'mystery centres', but perhaps places of basic teaching) were by the early sixth century being transformed into teaching centres for the expanding Celtic church, with the co-operation of 'Arthur' and all concerned. Dyfrig himself founded further monasteries at Llan Guorboe (unlocated) and Much (Moch?) Dewchurch, only a mile or so from Gamber head, before he retired to Bardsey in 537. From these centres spread the early foundations of the Welsh church, their many oratories of the different sizes which Nennius must have met on his travels. The main centre of the church then passed with St David (said by Gerald of Wales to be an 'uncle' of Arthur) to Dyfed, as Erging was vacated before the Saxons.

It was not until 597 that Augustine arrived from Rome to convert the Saxon invaders, which the Welsh church had not attempted to do. It is significant that he tried from the start to subjugate rather than co-operate with his supposed brothers of the Celtic church, and that his failure was reported as due to his arrogance in not even rising to greet them when they met at Aust in 602. Whereas Columba had achieved union in Ireland as early as 535, Northern England did not submit to Rome until 664 (Synod of Whitby), Wales until 717, and Cornwall not until the middle of the ninth century. It horrifies modern thought to find Bede still writing in 731 with approval of the slaughter of nearly 1200 unarmed British monks at Bangor-on-Dee, just because they had come to pray for the success of the British against the invasion of Wales from Northumbria.

Thereby the esoteric spirituality which had flowed into the Celtic church from the mysteries was brought to an end, here as elsewhere, by Rome.

3. Dissemination of the Legends

R. S. Loomis has concluded[8] that 'everything in the history of

Arthurian romance fits in with the view that legends, originating in Wales and Cornwall, were through the agency of professional reciters passed on to the bilingual Breton *conteurs*, who before 1100 had begun to fascinate audiences wherever French was understood.'

Yet the dates assigned by scholars to the story of *Culhwch*, the poem *Preiddeu Annwn*, and a few other fragments, indicate that written texts of these had been in existence for the best part of a century at least, without knowledge of them having become widespread. There seem to be three stages involved. The first is to form the item of mystery knowledge concerned into an imaginative picture which can really come alive in human souls; the initiative for this must come from those responsible within the mystery school. The second is to give this picture literary form, at first verbally and later in writing. The third is to make it available more generally, including translation into other languages. The three Brythonic languages of Welsh, Cornish and Breton had already grown apart.

We may ask why the decision to disseminate—for such there must have been—was taken when it was. The answer must have something to do with the fact that the Normans pressed into South Wales soon after the Conquest, and William himself visited St Davids before his death in 1085. Translation from Welsh to French had thus become a flourishing profession. Anticipating that the mysteries would be entirely suppressed, it was seen as important to transmute certain wisdom into legends suitable to catch and hold the attention of spiritually unsophisticated people, to lie in their souls as seeds which might germinate in a subsequent incarnation. To uplift Welsh morale may have been an extra incentive.

Three authors of romances give a similar name to their source: Chrestien refers to Bleheris, the author of the 'Elucidation' to Blihis, and Gottfried to Breri; Gerald of Wales also speaks of Blettri as a famous dealer in fables, and the poet Phylip Brydydd of Bleiddriw. For some decades prior to 1116 the Norman castle at Carmarthen—a port readily accessible to Brittany—was in the hands of a knight named Bleddri ap Kedivoc, known in Latin as Bledericus Latimeni, meaning 'the interpreter'. It seems probable that it was through him that around 1095 certain Arthurian themes were made known to a select group of Breton *conteurs*.

No written version in Breton has survived, and the process there seems to have been entirely oral. Taken hold of by the lively Breton imagination, combined both with Irish tales of an otherwordly nature and a heritage of stories carried by the Celts from their origins in Asia, transformed and embroidered, the results were shaped into Romance literature. Thence they were carried south to the courts of Italy (a tympanum at Modena is dated to 1100), east to Asia (by 1170), north to Scandinavia, and back through England (where many Breton households had accompanied William the Conqueror), to Wales itself. The absence of any mention of Arthur from the 'Lives' of the Breton saints, including those who had emigrated from England, indicates that he was not originally a living influence there. Yet by 1125 William of Malmesbury could write 'This is the Arthur concerning whom the idle tales of the Bretons rave wildly, even today.'

When Geoffrey of Monmouth wrote his influential *History of the Kings of Britain*, completed about 1136, he clearly took the greatest interest in the section on Arthur, devoting to it nearly a quarter of the whole, and even adding the name of Arthur to his own. He mentions a source book in the 'British' language, and the names he uses—Gorlois, Ridcaradoc, Dimilioc, Modredus, etc.—are Cornish in form. Geoffrey was a layman, probalby of Breton stock, and an ambitious man seeking preferment. Knowing that the church was opposed to Arthur, he produced a materialistic and pseudo-factual narrative, throwing in a few 'marvels' for effect. The result was to drag the spiritual reality down into a martial context, a deed typical of the work of Ahriman, the adversary spirit (Chapter 4.2). Such was the widespread longing to hear anything of

Arthur that his work was brilliantly successful. His clerical masters were well pleased, rewarding him with ordination in 1152 and consecration as Bishop of St Asaph a week later! But he probably never saw his see, which was in the hands of the rebellious Owein Gwynded until his death in 1155.

The works of Marie de France, (c. 1170) claim to be adapted from Breton lays; but she is said to show little knowledge of that language, and may well have written them in England. She goes to the opposite extreme—the element of 'faerie' is very pronounced, the dramatic interest is weak, and Arthur and his court serve only as a very shadowy background to the marvellous deeds of the heroes, Launval, Gawain or Tristan.

It is valuable to compare the *Erec et Enide* of Chrestien de Troyes (c. 1170) with the Welsh *Gereint*, and his *Yvain* (1176) with Owein. One can here experience directly the evolution of human consciousness. The Welsh versions, despite French accretions, still speak out of the immediate primitive forces which it was the task of the Arthurian mysteries to bring over from the megalithic age; they are direct, sensory in image, dramatic and to the point, set in a primitive society, yet filled with spirituality. The French versions express the same stories, incident for incident, but do so out of the subsequent age of the classical tradition as it lived on in France: they are relatively verbose, sensuous, set in a more formal courtly society, the spirituality more veiled. The subsequent work of Chrestien will be considered later (Chapter 7.3).

The authors of the *Mabiogion* are unknown, but it is thought likely that the Arthurian tales were composed in Erging.[9] The region retained its Welsh identity down to the twelfth century, and traditions from the age of Dyfrig seem to have been carried down. A Cornish influence there may be indicated by the number of farmsteads beginning with 'tre-'. At the same time, it was a region where Normans and Welsh, English and Bretons all met, and therefore a good place for the legends of one culture to spread into another.

4. Sources of the Grail Legend

We can only touch on this vast theme sufficiently to contrast it with the Arthurian stream. The Grail legend first became known through Robert de Boron (c. 1199).[10] He said that the vessel of the Last Supper was given to Pilate who, anxious to be rid of it, gave it, together with the permission to bury Christ's body, to Joseph of Arimathea. As he washed the body the blood flowed afresh and was caught in the vessel, which he hid. Joseph was blamed for the disappearance of the body, and imprisoned. Christ appeared to him in prison in a great light, and gave him anew the vessel, which shall be called the chalice, with instructions for its future care and the administration of the sacrament. All who see the chalice shall be of Christ's company, and have fulfilment of their heart's desire and joy eternal. (Robert adds: I dare not tell this, had I not the great book wherein are written the great secrets that are called the Grail.)

Joseph, nourished by the chalice, is at last released and sets off with his company to distant lands. He is instructed by the Holy Ghost to set the chalice openly before the people, and to recall the betrayal and the Last Supper, when Judas vacated his seat. He is to prepare another table, and Bron, his brother-in-law, is sent to catch a fish; this is put on the table with the chalice, which is covered. Joseph is to sit where Christ sat, with Bron on his right, after a vacant seat. The people are called; those who have faith in the Trinity and have kept Christ's commandment are invited to sit, and are so filled with sweetness and the desire of their heart that they forget their companions; the others feel nothing: the vessel thus severs the sinners from the fortunate. The chalice is named the 'Graal'. Moyses, a sinner, sits in the vacant seat and the earth swallows him up.

In course of time Joseph tells Bron's twelfth son, Alain, all about Christ's suffering and death, his own imprisonment, and the chalice, which he is shown; and he is given religious instruction to impart to others. Alain is to go West as far as possible, preaching Christ. The chalice is then given over to Bron, whose name is to be 'The Rich Fisher', and he too is to go westward, where he must wait for Alain's son, to whom the chalice and the grace that accompanies it are to be transmitted in turn. Joseph confides and expounds to the Rich Fisher alone, the words spoken to him by Christ in prison, sweet and precious, gracious and merciful, which are properly called the Secrets of the Grail, and are committed to writing. After three days the Rich Fisher goes forth, but Joseph remained in the land where he was born. (The poet then turned to the theme of Merlin.)

The Grail is here a vessel of grace, which imparts only spiritual delights to those who may sit at its table. The connection of the dish of the Last Supper with Joseph comes from Robert, not from any extant tradition. The Grail is the symbol of Christ's body, present at the Last Supper, brought to Pilate, received by Joseph, concealed, and reappearing with the risen Christ. It also symbolizes the Eucharist.

What were the Secrets of the Grail? A partial answer is found in a remarkable manuscript[11] mentioned by Heliandus (1204) as preserved by certain French nobles. It dates from the eighth century, and is thought to be genuine. It describes the initiation of an unnamed hermit living in 'the loneliest and wildest region of bright Britain' (which may also be Brittany or Ireland) at Easter 750. In the following brief summary, the stages have been numbered to show a rough correspondence to the Arthurian stages already described; but the mood is totally different—these are not 'battles' but deeply devotional feelings.

i) When the hermit meditates on Maundy Thursday on the arrest of Christ, he frees himself from the corruptible body and experiences in direct revelation a light-form of indescribable beauty, who breathes upon him with the words 'I am the great Master, the source of all certitude and all wisdom', and reaches to him a 'book' the size of a man's hand, saying: 'In it are my secrets, written in my own hand. He who reads it rightly will find his heart freed from all suffering, and filled with all joy that the heart can receive.' ii)The first chapter of this book shows the hermit his spiritual lineage (i.e., the Grail succession) and he feels how far he has fallen short of this—an experience of the Guardian. iii) The second contains 'the book of the holy Grail', and iv) the third contains 'the horrors'. v) Only after this can the fourth chapter, 'the marvels', be approached. There is a ray of flaming fire that strikes like lightning, but continues to grow and is terrifying. Then vi) the sun becomes as dark as night for a while, and afterwards there comes a sweet-scented breeze, and a mighty paeon of praise to the bringer of eternal life is heard from innumerable invisible voices; this alternates seven times with a sounding of bells, and then vanishes. The hermit is then reminded to perform the service appointed for Good Friday. vii) As he makes the three parts of the sacrament he is prevented by an Angel, who leads him to a level above the third heaven described by St Paul, which is 'a hundred times clearer than glass'. Here (at the stage where Arthur 'carried the cross') he beholds the divine Trinity separated into three Persons and in living movement again becoming One. St John rightly says that no mortal can see this, but as spirit freed from the body it can be beheld. Returning to the previous level, an innumerable heavenly host falls to the ground around the majesty. As the Angel lays him again in his body he has the power to make intelligible the Being of the Trinity, and after completing the service locks the little book in a shrine before taking nourishment.

When he seeks the book again on Easter Sunday it is gone, 'as Jesus was gone from the grave'. Now begins a wandering totally different from the Arthurian path.

A) The first day he passes through the Valley of the Dead to the Junction of Seven Roads, and comes to the Spring of Tears 'where the great slaughter was' (the realm of the intellect). Here he meets his animal guide, with a white lamb's head, a black dog's limbs, the trunk of a chestnut horse, and the tail of a lion. He is led through dense woods to the hut

of a hermit, a 'good man' who thinks only good of others.
B) On the second day he reaches the Fir of Adventure, under which is a second spring, its gravel red and hot, its water icy, three times a day turning emerald-green and bitter (a rhythmic process, suggesting man's rhythmic system). Here he is sent food and drink by 'she whom the knight with the gold circlet saved from destruction the day the great marvel was seen'. He is accommodated by a knight who knows his youth.

C) On the third day he comes to a meadow called 'The Lake of the Queen', with a nunnery. At dusk he approaches a chapel when he hears a horrible cry, and finds a hermit unconscious in the entrance, who is possessed by the devil himself. He tries to exorcise it in Christ's name, but the devil proves that he has not the power to do so. But on the altar he finds the little book, by which the devil and his hosts are driven out below (the 'dragon' in the metabolic system). He watches over the hermit for nine days, receiving divine food daily at a third spring.

D) Finally he returns home, and has until Ascension to copy the little book, which will then ascend to heaven.

The manuscript thus describes the purification of the soul, vision of the Trinity, and then experience of the Trinity in the threefold human body. The 'little book' again represents the Word, the body of Christ which is laid in the grave at Easter and vanishes at Ascension. It is the gift of the living Christ, to be found again in depths of adversity when Christ is invoked at the centre of evil.

5. The Two Streams Merge

Up to the eighth century the Arthurian centre in Wales, perhaps at Byrdd Arthur in Anglesey, continued to lead pupils from the study of nature to living experience of the elemental beings springing forth from mineral, plant, animal and human kingdoms like an aura fertilized out of the cosmos. They experienced the earth element in its gravity, the water in its life-giving quality, the air in its power to awaken sentient consciousness, and fire in its power to kindle the 'I'. Directing all this, as a living being in her full radiance, appeared to them Creiddylad, the metamorphosed Ceridwen or Persephone, ever-creating beneath the earth in Gwyn's kingdom in winter, above the earth in Gwythyr's kingdom in summer—the experience of the course of the year of an earlier age (Chapter 2.3) still echoing on in a vivid way. But now, since the descent of Christ had been experienced in the realm of the elements (Chapter 4.1), this goddess of Nature was felt as the handmaid of Christ, the Sun Being.

They learned still to know the further path into the planetary world, described in Chapter 3, and how their own soul in its sevenfold nature works and weaves and lives. They learned, too, the path onward to the 'Great Ocean' of the fixed stars, described in Chapter 4, when they penetrated to the nature of the 'I'. Amid all this was experienced the etheric working of Christ as cosmic Sun-Being.

Meanwhile Christ Himself, who had descended to earth in the East, gained recognition increasingly across Europe towards the West, working within the hearts of men. In the sixth century the Celtic church had spread from Britain and Ireland to Scotland, North England and the continent, as far as Switzerland; whilst the church centred on Rome continued its spread westwards. We have seen how these two outer garments of Christ met here in the seventh and eighth centuries.

Rudolf Steiner has described[12] how, during the ninth century, the inner realities—Christ Himself, the Brother of Humanity from the East, and His cosmic working as Sun-Being in the etheric world from the West—also came together. Thereby the Arthurian stream, which had flourished in the West for 2000 years, came together with the Grail stream springing from the Event in Palestine, which was destined to work on into the future. It was, at the same time, at the 8th

Ecumenical Council of 869 that the Roman church formed the dogma proscribing the threefold concept of body, soul and spririt, and asserting that 'man has only a spiritual soul gifted with reason', from which all modern dualism derives. But an esoteric Christianity which sustained the Trinity in man's nature as fundamental (and was thus made heretical) continued to live in the merging of the Arthurian and Grail streams.

These streams can be traced further, as Steiner also pointed out,[13] in the School of Chartres, which flourished between 1000 and 1200, just before the present cathedral was built (1195-1225). There were still times when Christ was conceived as the cosmic Sun Spirit Who had appeared in Jesus of Nazareth, although His impulse was also received in the sense of the Grail conception; but this cannot be supported from surviving texts. A teacher named Peter of Compostella still spoke of the Goddess Natura as the handmaid of Christ: only when Natura has introduced a pupil to the elements, the planetary world, and the world of stars, he said, is he ripe to become acquainted in very reality of soul with the seven Goddesses of the Liberal Arts—Grammatica, Dialectica, Rhetorica; Musica, Arithmetica, Geometrica and Astronomica—whom he came to know as divine-spiritual Beings, living and real. Bernard of Chartres (d. 1130) could no longer lead his pupils to see these Goddesses, but spoke of them so livingly that Imagined pictures of them were still conjured up. Bernardus Silvestris (fl 1147) could give only mighty and powerful descriptions. The pupils of John of Salisbury (d. 1180) merely knew about them. And Alanus ab Insulis (d. 1203), who spoke directly out of spiritual vision with true enthusiasm and inspiration, saw that such teachings could no longer be given at all.

Meanwhile, during the tenth and eleventh centuries the declining Arthurian centre in Wales had performed its final spiritual deed—the clothing of some of its wisdom in legendary form. During the twelfth and the beginning of the thirteenth centuries this was taken up and reshaped into the written form that has come down to us. The year 1250 was a turning-point

in human consciousness, when there was for a time no clairvoyance at all on earth.[14] The impetus which had given rise
not only to the legends, but to the great period of construction of cathedrals and churches, had petered out.

When we next hear of Arthur in Britain, it is not in a spiritual
context but in a political one. The 'discovery' of Arthur's grave
was a political move to support the claim of Edward I to be
the successor of this celebrated but mortal figure; and it is
significant that this took place at Glastonbury, the centre of
Arthur's opponent Melwas, and sponsored by the Roman
church. Meanwhile, pageants transformed the Round Table
into a species of entertainment, which became popular between 1250 and 1350. The reality had vanished and, despite
the efforts of Malory (1485), the legends came to be seen as
mere make-believe.

CHAPTER SEVEN

CHRONICLERS AND ROMANCERS

1. Geoffrey of Monmouth

Geoffrey wrote his influential *History of the Kings of Britain*,[1] completed about 1136, on the basis of existent chronicles and king-lists, especially the writings of Gildas, Bede and Nennius, and also mentions a source-book in the 'British' language. On this factual skeleton he created a work of literary fantasy from his own fertile imagination, and nowhere was this more the case than in relation to Arthur, whose story he expanded to form almost a quarter of the whole. He was the first to write of 'King' Arthur—in direct contradiction to Nennius, as we saw in Chapter 2.6—and to depict him as a military leader charging aggressively not only across Britian but across the whole of Northern Europe. This corresponded to a deep need in the human soul. Historians and archaeologists have obligingly created a 'historical' Arthur of the fifth-sixth centuries to match, so far as Britain is concerned, but there is no basis for connecting their very real findings with the name of Arthur. That Geoffrey deliberately misconstrued his sources for his personal benefit has already been suggested (Chapter 6.3), and although his work was copied by many others to form a group of manuscripts known as the 'Chronicles', it is significant that the main stream of continental Romances took no account of the pseudo-historical framework he invented. In

Welsh tradition Arthur appears as a 'chief prince' (Triad 1), but more often as an otherworldly ruler. Geoffrey was also the first written source to connect the name of Merlin with Arthur, confusing in the process Merlin Ambrosius, magician to Vortigern, with Myrddin Wyllt, poet and prophet to Gwenddolau on the Scottish border (Chapter 5.3).

He begins his section on Arthur in the traditional way with a birth-story, which is not found in earlier Welsh tradition, although Gruffyd[2] considered that there is 'an overwhelmingly strong case that it is based on Welsh material'. What we have here is a story of Merlin using magic on the physical plane to deceive an innocent lady in order to satisfy the lascivious desires of a lusting tyrant. But in this form it is not at all in keeping with Welsh tradition, where we have seen (Chapter 3.6) that shape-shifting belongs to the elemental world, not to the physical. If we seek the Imagination that Geoffrey has debased, we may come upon the following:

Gorlois, Duke of Cornwall and 'a man of great experience and mature years', advises the king on a night attack against the Saxons, which is successful; he represents the ancient moon-wisdom based on the blood stream. At Easter (when the Divine Spirit suffers death and the sense-world burgeons) the king celebrates the feast, and is filled with desire for Ygerna, wife of Gorlois; Utherpendragon, 'terrible head dragon', represents the opponent of St Michael, namely the desires and lower passions devoted to the sense-world consequent on the Fall, who seeks to seduce the soul from knowledge of the spirit. Gorlois, 'more worried about his wife than himself', withdraws without leave and places Ygerna in Tintagel 'until he could receive help from Ireland', and takes refuge in a fort five miles away. Tintagel being impregnable, Uther sends for Merlin who, by 'methods which are quite new and until now unheard of', gives Uther the precise appearance of Gorlois: personal, intellectual thinking, which first emerged in the fifth century as a common faculty, makes knowledge of the sense-world appear as wisdom. Uther, the sense-world, is thus enabled to seduce Ygerna, the original 'generative power' ('eigyr') of the soul, and Gorlois, the ancient wisdom, is killed. Arthur is born of the union; the Arthurian mysteries are earth mysteries, but also carry over some of the ancient star-wisdom into a later age. Geoffrey depicts the young Arthur, 'of outstanding courage and generosity' being chosen as king at puberty, and bustling about Britain, defending it against Saxons in the east, Picts and Scots in the north, and then eliminating an Irish invading force. His marriage to 'Ganhumare' (Gwenhwyvar) is briefly described. Then comes a very odd insertion about three lakes: Loch Lomond, having exactly sixty islands, feeder streams, crags and eagles (earth, water, air); a nearby pool, twenty-feet square, with different fish remaining in each corner; and a pool near the Severn which swallows the sea without overflowing, then belches it forth as high as a mountain (the Severn bore?)— anyone facing this is in danger of being swallowed up, but not if he turns his back. The point of such improbable 'marvels', totally without context, is not apparent, unless it be to pour scorn on otherworld descriptions.

The third section opens with Arthur's conquest of Ireland and Iceland. After twelve years of peace he then sails against Norway and Denmark, returning through Gaul. After another nine years he gives Normandy to Bedevere (Bedwyr), Anjou to Kay (Cei), and returns to celebrate his mastery of the nor- thern world at Caerleon. This whole description is, historically, nonsense in the sixth century, or at any time since, perhaps, the spread of the Celts in the fourth century BC. But the area described is precisely that of the Northern mysteries of Sig. Each initiate who was to hold the rank of 'Arthur' would have had to master both the Irish (Hybernian) mysteries and these Northern mysteries in acquiring his full initiation.

The fourth section deals with Arthur's struggle with Rome, in detail which must be fictional; but that such conflict existed in a spiritual sense is amply confirmed. The section starts with another incongruous 'marvel', that of Arthur killing a pig-eating Spanish giant on Mont St Michel—a strange way of expressing

Arthur's connection with St Michael and the pig-mysteries!
After two skirmishes near Autun the Roman army is defeated
at Soissy. Up to this point twelve knights had been named:
Cador of Cornwall and Hoel of Brittany; Loth and his sons
Gawain (Gwalchmei) and Mordred; Bedevere and Kay; Urien,
Augulselsus, Boso, Gerin and Hyderus (Ider), son of Nu (Nudd).
There is no suggestion that this was a conscious listing of the
Round Table, but it might be so. Another twenty names occur
during the battle.

Arthur is about to advance on Rome itself when he learns
of treachery at home. We return to Welsh sources for this last
section. Mordred, left in charge of the kingdom, had seized
the throne and abducted Ganhumare. When Arthur returns she
flees to the City of the Legions and becomes a nun. Arthur
fights skirmishes at Richborough (where Gawain is killed), and
Winchester, before the fatal battle on the river Camblan in
Cornwall, at which Mordred was killed. Arthur, mortally
wounded himself, hands the crown to Cador's son (i.e., he
restores the lineage of Cornwall) before he is 'carried off to
the isle of Avalon so that his wounds might be attended to.'
His burial is not mentioned, as might have been expected, so
that his future is left open.

2. Wace and Layamon

The first important adaptation of Geoffrey's story was that of
Wace, who rewrote it in Norman-French verse at Caen about
1155.[3] He followed the same sequence, but gave it a courtly
grace, and added stories about Arthur, Gawain and Merlin, probably from Breton sources. He even went to the fountain in
Barenton in the forest of Broceliande, and was disappointed
not to see the marvel that he expected. He tells how 'the
minstrel has sung his ballad, the storyteller told his tale so frequently, little by little he has decked and painted, till by reason
of his embellishments the truth stands hid in the trappings of

a tale'—fair comment on Romance literature, but a false
implication that his own chronicle is 'the truth'.
Wace was the first to write of a physical Round Table, 'of
which the Bretons tell many a tale'. He adds that 'all were
seated within the circle, and no one was placed outside the
Round Table', which suggests a small community looking outwards towards the circle of the heavens; but in keeping with
his whole tendency to exaggerate, many more than twelve
knights are named. Round tables, as such, were nothing new.
Thus Posidonius (c.90 BC) reported: 'The Celts banquet around
wooden tables slightly elevated above ground, and when many
are assembled they sit in a circle, the bravest in the middle like
the leader of a chorus, because he is superior to the rest either
in military skill, or in birth, or in riches; and the man who gives
the entertainment sits next to him, and then on each side the
rest of the guests according as each is eminent or distinguished
for anything.' Since primitive Irish architecture was circular,
circular seating there would be inevitable.[4] Arthurian adventures usually began whilst the knights were 'eating', i.e., receiving spiritual nourishment from outside their totality.
    It is also Wace who adds after Arthur's mortal wound at the
battle on the Camel: 'He is yet in Avalon, awaited of the
Britons; for as they say and deem, he will return from whence
he went and live again. . . Men have ever doubted—and, as
I am persuaded, will always doubt—whether he lives or is
dead.' William of Malmesbury had already written in 1125
(thus before Geoffrey) of 'The Breton hope of Arthur's return',
as well as of Arthur as 'a man certainly worthy to be celebrated
in truthful histories, since for a long time he sustained the
declining fortunes of his native land, and incited the uncrushed
courage of his people to war'—compatible as much with
spiritual leadership as with generalship.
    The last important chronicle following Geoffrey, though
there were many others, was that of Layamon, a parish priest
from Arley on Severn, above Worcester, who about 1190
transformed Wace's story into prolix English verse that is less

courtly, more direct.[3] He exults over Celtic triumphs and must have drawn on a Welsh source—he uses older forms such as Walwain for Gwalchmei, Wenhafer for Gwenhwyvar. Of Arthur's birth he adds: 'So soon as he came on earth, elves took him; they enchanted the child with magic most strong.' Arthur was for him nevertheless a very real monarch, cruel to his foes and stern to his own men. The Round Table becomes a portable affair to seat sixteen-hundred, 'without and within, man against man'.

Layamon incorporates a dream of Arthur after hearing of Mordred's treachery: 'I began to wander wide over the moors; there I saw gripes, and grisly fowls! Then approached a golden lion over the down. . . and took me by the middle. . . and in the sea went with myself. . . The waves took her from me; but there approached a fish and brought me to land'—not inappropriate before the last mortal encounter.

To the story of Arthur's end he adds: 'There came from the sea a short boat, floating with the waves, and two women in it, wondrously fair, who took Arthur quickly and laid him softly down, and departed. Merlin prophesied he should return. . . Bruttes (Britons) ileveth yet that he beon live, and wunnion in Avalon mid fairest alre alven (elves); and lokieth evere Bruttes yet when Arthur comen lithe.' Awareness of the elemental world, at least, was still a reality. From this first telling in English, Malory, Spenser and many others drew in turn.

3. Chrestien de Troyes

The work of Chrestien marks a turning-point in Arthurian literature. It ignores the materialistic pattern of Geoffrey and Wace, and although speaking of 'King' Arthur remains firmly set in the otherworld. His *Erec et Enide*[5] (1170) follows and elaborates the same source as the Welsh *Gereint* (Chapter 4.2), but mentions in passing the names of Lancelot of the Lake, Perceval of Wales, Gornemant of Gohort and the Round Table.

Arthur's court is at Tintagel when Erec succeeds his father as king of Farther Wales (Cornwall). At this coronation by Arthur, Erec's robe, made by four fairies, bears representations of geometry, arithmetic, music and astronomy, the 'quadrivium' of Chartres and other centres of learning, into which Arthurian wisdom had flowed (Chapter 6.5).

Chrestian says that he wrote of Iseult and King Mark, but this is not extant, and it was probably given up when Thomas pre-empted the theme with his *Tristan*. His *Cliges* (1176) is a double love story of father and son, linked at intervals to Arthur's court, but in its whole mood of quite different provenance. It is based on a French model, and has been called an 'anti-Tristan'.[5] It is significant that one scene reflects the passion and resurrection of Christ. In the final tournament Cliges defeats Sagramor, Lancelot and Perceval, and his contest with Gawain is ended only by Arthur's intervention.

In his *Yvain* (1177) Chrestien elaborates the same source as the Welsh *Owein*, which we saw in Chapter 5.1 to depict the path out to the sun-sphere and the return to a new incarnation. The big black man, keeper of the forest (now the forest of Broceliande in Brittany) has here a head bigger than that of a horse, with ears like an elephant, eyes like an owl, a nose like a cat, a jowl like a wolf, and teeth like a wild boar. The spring is of hot water, and the marble slab has become a stone of emerald, with rubies showing through. These features echo unmistakably the multicoloured animal guide and the second spring in the *Book of the Grail* (Chapter 6.4).

We consider next a short story, most probably by Chrestien, *The Mule without a Bridle*[6]. i) A maiden approaches Arthur's court on a mule with only a halter, and offers her love to whoever recovers her bridle: the mule will know the way. ii) Kay at once offers, and enters a vast forest. iii) He is much afraid of the many lions, tigers and leopards, but 'because of their knowledge of the lady, out of respect for her mule' they kneel before it. iv) A little path leads to an extremely perilous dark valley, with a north wind and all the hatefulness of winter, which contains enormous fire-breathing and stinking snakes, serpents and scorpions. v) He emerges safely onto a plain with a flowery meadow and a pure spring, where the mule is watered. vi) He then reaches a deep, wide and very black stream of turbulent water, and can find only a narrow plank across. Kay gives up here and returns in shame. Gawain repeats the adventure, and finds that the plank, though only two inches wide, is of iron, and puts the mule across. vii) He comes to a revolving castle, surrounded by a moat and stakes with heads on them, but as the door comes past he breaks in on the mule. He is met by a dwarf, and then by a churl from the cellars, who gives him food and lodging. A) The churl challenges him to the beheading game (cf., *Bricriu's Feast* and *Gawain and the Green Knight*), and he beheads the churl. Next morning the churl raises the axe to him, but leaves him untouched 'because he was so loyal'. B) At noon he has to face two lions, and needs seven shields before he has killed them. C) He now has to fight a knight previously wounded in body, whose wound is healed by his arrival, and Gawain defeats him. He still has to overcome two savage dragons. D) The dwarf then invites him to eat with the maiden's sister, from whom he receives the bridle. Many people come out of the cellars rejoicing as he returns to court.

We find here a development of the Book of the Grail (Chapter 6.4): the common path we already recognized to the sun-sphere, then the threefold experience of the body—the beheading game, renewing the head forces; the two lions, which always represent the sun-forces in the heart; the wounded knight and two dragons (limb-metabolic system); communion with the lady of the bridle, and freedom for others. An Arthurian knight thus achieves a Grail path to the point of receiving the bridle with which to control spiritual forces within the body (the mule).

Chrestien's *Knight of the Cart*[5] or *Lancelot* (1177) seems to be an original creation inspired from Grail sources and, as such, full analysis is beyond our present scope. It is set at Camelot at Ascension. To a challenge Arthur replies supinely that he must endure what he has not the power to change. Through the bravado and inadequacy of Kay, the queen is abducted by Meleagant (Melwas: Chapter 3.8) to 'the kingdom whence no foreigner returns'. Gawain sets out in pursuit and meets an unknown knight, who reaches the queen and is recognized by her as Lancelot. His adventures indicate the second half of the Grail path. A) Two horses die under him; he is carried in a cart, as is the head; he enters a tower on a rock, and receives a green mantle (the auric colour of thinking); thus far Gawain accompanies him. He is carried deep in thought across a plain. B) After forcing a ford he visits a lone damsel and receives a scarlet mantle: his loyalty is tested in defending her in her bedroom, and his chastity when she lies in his bed; deep feelings arise when they find a comb with the queen's hair; they reach the meadow of play and sport. C) He reaches the cemetery of destiny; with two youths he passes the stony passage and goes through a rocky fortress; he reaches the sword-bridge, never yet traversed, and in crossing injures hands, knees and feet, but disclaims feeling pain. D) He has various experiences with the queen, including the loss of blood in her bed, and finally kills the evil Meleagant. Meanwhile Gawain is saved from drowning at the water-bridge, tries to help Lancelot, but is precluded from doing so. The Arthurian impulse is supplanted by the Grail.

4. Peredur-Perceval-Parzival

The tale of *Peredur* (pronounced Perédir) in the *Mabinogion* is thought[7] to have been composed about 1135, probably in North Wales. The name means 'steel lances', but may originally have had common origin with that of Pryderi, whose character is similar. Chrestien de Troyes' *Perceval*[9] (c.1182) clearly drew from a similar source for a more sophisticated audience. Wolfram von Eschenbach's *Parzival*[10] (c.1215) follows the latter at a higher level of moral-spiritual discernment, with a prelude about the hero's father, and completes it where Chrestien breaks off. The tales begin similarly, following stages like those in Chapter 3 above, although in different pictures.

1) Each hero is the son of a widow, brought up in a forest. Each is quick and apt, but the only prenatal hint is that *Perceval* opens with bird-song, and Parzival weeps at the beauty of it as if it recalled memories.

2) Each sets out to be knighted, to his mother's mortal grief; Perceval alone looks back and sees her fall, and is hence the more blameworthy. They pass through desert, wilderness and forest. Their inner life is equally dead, for they take from the Lady of the Clearing food, a ring, and a kiss—Peredur with permission, Perceval roughly, Parzival dully—leaving her desolated. Parzival meets Sigune with a dead knight in her arms who had died fighting on his behalf, and pity awakens in him. At Arthur's court each is derided, but welcomed by two people, whom Cei chastises. The Red Knight has affronted Gwenhwyvar without challenge, but the hero kills him with a dart through the eye (death to the senses), and takes his horse and armour.

3) Each hero reaches the court of an uncle, Gurnemans, who instructs him in knighthood, but tells him not to ask questions—'may any guilt fall on me'. By thus restraining the lad, who is still immature, he assumes the role of Guardian of the Threshold.

4) There is here a variation in sequence and a major difference in quality of experience. Peredur reaches the hall of a second uncle, where a bleeding spear is carried past, followed by a bleeding head on a platter. Rudolf Steiner said of this:[8] 'The mysteries became decadent and were horribly profaned in the symbol of a dish on which a bleeding head had to be laid—what was at work here was nothing but black magic.' The cult of the severed head was widespread in Celtic society—the heads of defeated foes were regularly set on stakes at the entrance to a captured town. We find a similar demand

by Herodias for the head of John the Baptist, but the author is more likely to have had in mind that the head of Gruffyd ap Llewelyn, murdered by the English in 1063, had been sent to King Harold in London. The uncle continued his conversation, and Peredur asked no question.

In contrast, Perceval in the corresponding scene meets the Fisher King and enters the Grail castle, where in a sequence of five stages he is given a special sword and sees the Grail. This is 'of pure gold, with precious stones of diverse kinds' and 'shining with a splendid brightness', its shape unspecified. Perceval could hardly be expected to interrupt the conversation of the Fisher King to ask about his disability or about an undisclosed person. When he meets Sigune, who holds a decapitated corpse, her curse seems unjustified. Parzival's experience is, however, of a much more Imaginative character, the impressive ritual in the castle embodying in seven stages many secrets of number and planetary influences. He not only sees 'a thing called the Grail', the 'perfection of Paradise', tended by twenty-four maidens (Chapter 3.4), and receives what is clearly a magic sword, but also catches a glimpse of the ancient Titurel, and longs to ask about him, but obediently refrains. Sigune, now holding the embalmed body, a true *pietà*, now tells him who he is, and seems more justified in her curse. For both heroes the Grail seems to be a manifestation of divinity, as we found in Chapter 3.4 at this point.

At a castle reduced almost to starvation a maiden, Kondwiramurs, with black hair, white skin and red cheeks—the counterpart of Olwen (Chapter 3.4), though her hair was golden—comes to the hero by night pleading for help: to Peredur desperately, to Perceval almost to blackmail, to Parzival in purity. Each hero falls in love but remains chaste; Parzival alone marries Kondwiramurs.

5) The threefold confrontation with the Giant (Chapter 3.5) is echoed in the hero's battle with the leader of the beleaguering earl's retinue, his steward, and the earl himself (Clamide). Each hero then begins to set destiny aright by defeating the

Proud One of the Clearing, who in *Parzival* bears dragons on his helmet, his shield and his surcoat.

6) Peredur alone encounters the nine witches of Gloucester on entering the elementary world. He strikes one of them, and receives their training and takes their weapons and horse, but does not fully master them. Each hero then experiences drops of blood in the snow (and Peredur the blackness of a raven) as an Imagination of his beloved. Meanwhile Arthur's court have come in search of him, and after one or 24 (Peredur) knights have challenged him and been thrown, Cei does the same; he is injured, stopping him as usual at this point.

7) Gwalchmei/Gawain considers it wrong to disturb a meditation, covers the drops, and courteously invites him to Arthur's court, where he is warmly welcomed.

* * * * *

The next incidents, which happen to Peredur alone and follow the Arthurian sequence, continue into Chapter 4 above. He meets Angharad (Beloved) Goldenhair, but is rejected; his vow to speak to no Christian until he has won her re-echoes the silencing of Imaginations to make way for Inspirations.

8) He enters Round Valley, with uncouth black houses, representing the sun but with its sunspots. He first subdues a lion, the heart forces; after slaying many giants he grants mercy to others on condition of baptism, hinting at a connection of Christ with the sun sphere (Chapter 4.1). He then kills a serpent to acquire a ring of gold, symbol of the higher ego. Returning to court, he ignores an untimely injury from Cei, and in dumbly defeating an aggressor wins Angharad's love.

9) In confronting the Black Oppressor he asks a compassionate question: Who put your eye out? But this is the wrong situation, and it has a baneful result. He does however learn of the second aspect of evil, the Worm of the Barrow.

10) The three sons killed daily by the Addanc (cf., the Avanc— Chapter 2.2), and restored overnight, depict the daily

wear and tear on our soul-faculties of thinking, feeling and willing in day-consciousness and their restoration through sleep.
Given the stone of invisibility by a maiden from the East, he
passes a valley where sheep change from black to white as they
cross a river (the reversal on entering spiritland—(Chapter 4.4)
and sees a tree half green, half flame (the preservation of
balance). The Addanc is duly vanquished.

11) He reaches and slays the Worm of the Barrow, which
has a precious stone in its tail (as the black witch was the
daughter of the white witch—Chapter 4.3)—the transforming
of evil leads to new good. 12) He comes to the land of windmills (the lotus flowers revolve when activated—Chapter 4.4)
and rules for 14 years with the empress of Constantinople
(whence the Cymry claimed to originate—Chapter 2.2).

As an Arthurian sequence the tale should finish here; but
there are added—probably later—some garbled incidents from
the Grail sequence (below), the coming of Cundrie, the battle
in the tower, the Good Friday meeting with a priest, and the
Castle of Wonders, for which three meaningless incidents are
invented. Then the 'marvels' are trivially explained away. To
master the nine witches of Gloucester, Arthur himself is finally
invoked.

We may conclude that this tale was written by someone
acquainted with the path of the Arthurian mysteries, but that
this was not only misunderstood but actually transformed to
evil at several crucial points. The Arthurian stream must have
become decadent by 1100 for this to occur.

* * * * *

The tales of *Perceval* and *Parzival* take on a quite different
dramatic sequence, which we may recognize as that of the Grail
stream. A girl of extreme ugliness, whose description may
remind us of the multi-coloured beast that guided the hermit
(Chapter 6.4) curses the hero for not asking about the bleeding
lance and 'what worthy man was served from the Grail'. A

knight then enters and accuses Gawain of treachery, which he denies but undertakes to defend in forty days before the king of Esc-avalon. Both leave at once. Gawain comes first to Tintagel 'for there was no other way to go', and reluctantly joins a tournament only when a small girl implores him to champion her. In *Parzival* this is a battle, and he is on the attacking side: whereas Gawain fights evil, Parsifal enters into it in order to transform it.

A) At Escavalon Gawain is invited to a tower (the head), but when he dallies with the hostess the townspeople attack, and he defends the door with a chessboard whilst she hurls chessmen (thoughts). The king, who owes him safe passage, frees them on his return, but he must fetch the lance (*Perceval*) or Grail (*Parzival*) which Parzival had required of the king.

Whereas Wolfram had allowed several years between Parzival's first and second visits to Arthur's court, during which he had matured enormously, Chrestien had allowed Perceval only forty days. But now we learn that Perceval had wandered for five years 'without a thought for God'. Both heroes spend Good Friday with a hermit, brother to the Fisher King, and learn that their failure is due to their sin against their mother. Perceval is merely enjoined to go daily to church, and is taught a prayer containing 'many of the names of Our Lord'. But Parzival (who had acquired a Grail horse) learns that the Grail is 'a stone fallen from heaven'—its secrets had been read in the stars; and he learns of the family which guards the Grail, to which he himself belongs—it is thus an impulse related to the blood stream and the human heart. Both make confession and receive communion.

B) Gawain is warned of danger by a wounded knight, but is entranced by a haughty girl, and against much advice fetches her palfrey. He brings a herb that heals the knight, who promptly steals his horse, much to her amusement; and he has to follow her on a nag until he recovers it. He sees a fine castle with many ladies across a river, and, lodging with a boatman, learns that it is protected by magic. He enters the hall and sits on a gold bed, whereupon seven-hundred arrows smash against his shield (and in *Parzival* the bed cannons around the room). He is then attacked by a lion, which he kills. He is lovingly tended, and welcomed by a queen, but told he may not leave. When, however, next morning he sees, from a turret, the haughty girl, he crosses back to her. Parzival, too, has been to the castle, but was not entranced by the girl and did not undergo the trials in the hall.

C) Gawain is tempted to the Perilous Ford, where he fails the leap, but scrambles ashore with his horse. He is challenged by Gramoflanz, lord of the castle, and learns that the queen is Arthur's mother and another queen his own mother, both long dead. Gramoflanz demands revenge for an old affront, and Gawain sends for Arthur as witness.

Chrestien's work finishes here in mid-sentence. The stages of the Grail path have been indicated: the battle in the tower, the head; emotional entanglement and the Castle of Wonders, the heart; and the leap, demanding strength of limb. The Grail path leads to deep understanding of the miracle of Man. The work of the Continuators is mere fiction compared to this.

*   *   *   *   *

Now the real mystery of Parzival begins. He encounters Gawain 'by mischance', gains the upper hand, and cries 'It is I myself whom I have vanquished'; he regains control of his destiny. Indeed he takes upon himself Gawain's battle with Gramoflanz. In another encounter he meets his rich half-brother from the East, Feirefiz, who is partly black and partly white—various polarities of light and darkness in Wolfram's tale point to a Manichean influence.

Cundrie now appears to proclaim Parzival Lord of the Grail. Significantly he takes not Gawain but his eastern brother, his second self, to the Grail castle. As Cundrie says, he has at last attained soul's peace, the state of blessedness (*Saelde*). He at once asks Amfortas, not the question which concerned

Perceval about the nature of the lance and the Grail, but the more human question, 'Uncle, what troubles you?' Through Him who is present when two or three are together in such a way, Amfortas is at once healed; such working through the Word as sacramental deed forecasts the future.

At last Parzival is reunited with Kondwiramurs, and their younger son is crowned king of all his lands. The elder accompanies them to the Grail, which again provides sustenance as before. Later, after he has been trained in the Grail's service, the latter is sent to carry the impulse of the Grail out into the world.

It may be added that Stein[11] has shown that during the Arthurian stages Wolfram has secreted pictures indicating the sequence of the constellations of the zodiac. And Teutschmann[12] has shown that the scene in Trevrezent's cell represents an initiation into the successive planetary forces, which Cundrie later names. Here we have a last echo of the wisdom of the cosmos brought over by the Arthurian mysteries from earlier ages. Arthur himself 'returns to Camelot'. But the secret of Parzival is that, as ex-Arthurian and Lord of the inner world of the Grail, this wisdom of the cosmos begins to shine out anew from within him.

5. Thomas Malleorré

A period of 260 years lies between Wolfram's *Parzival*—with Gottfired von Strassburg's *Tristan*, the last of the great esoteric legends—and Malleorreś compilation[13] published in 1485. During this time the so-called 'Arthurian legends', and the characters in them, proliferated vastly, especially in France: but in fact Arthur and his impulse became a mere backdrop. The main interest centred in Lancelot and his adultery with Gwenyvere, which in reality was meant to picture the transition of the soul from the Arthurian to the Grail mysteries. Not only had the Arthurian mysteries ceased to be a creative element long before, but the spark of esotericism itself had passed over from the troubadours and poets to the Templars and the Rosicrucians. Esoteric legends were consequently supplanted by works of fiction.

When, therefore, Malleorré undertook his task of bringing as many tales as he could get hold of into a single framework, he was unfortunately dealing with some manuscrips which incorporated genuine wisdom from the Grail stream, but with many others which did not. The choice of subject and high moral tone and purpose of this work does not seem to tally with what is known of the soldier and hardened malefactor, Thomas Malory, who died in 1471, and it is still questioned whether Sir Thomas Malleorré—as he himself spells his name—has been rightly identified. Henry Tudor, who came to the throne in the year Caxton published, felt himself to be a descendant of Arthur, names his eldest son Arthur, and founded an Order of Arthur, and an associate from the North of England imprisoned in France and writing to prepare the way for him, would seem much more probable.

The first section, 'The Tale of King Arthur', is a collection of incidents, one or two of which contain a flash of Arthurian substances. For example, Arthur chases the hart that was the quest of Pellinor (Beli Mawr, the great Belinus—Chapter 2.4), challenges him, and is defeated, being only rescued by the intervention of Merlin. The Celtic invaders did indeed carry the worship of Belinus to the greater part of Britain, and Arthurian influence only survived in Cornwall and Wales under the influence of the Arthurian mysteries founded by Merlin. Or again, Arthur had images made in stone of twelve kings who had died, with himself standing above them with drawn sword, and a taper burning 'until the Sankgreall was achieved'. Here is a last picture of the spiritual Round Table in its true size, which in the chronicles and romances had grown bigger and bigger; but it is rigidified in stone.

'The Tale of the Noble king Arthur' is only a further elaboration on Geoffrey of Monmouth. 'The Noble Tale of Sir

Lancelot' is no more than a sequence of most improbable fictions. 'The Tale of Sir Gareth' indeed contains valuable elements of a Grail legend, but it is not Arthurian. 'The Book of Sir Tristam' is an overlong and pedestrian extravaganza based on characters from the real Tristan and Grail legends, which it thereby debases.

The well-known 'Tale of the Sankgreall' is based on a Cistercian fable, 'The Quest of the Holy Grail' (c.1225), which was designed to divert the individual's search for inner reality back towards a sanctimonious morality within the purview of the church. The whole matter of inner development and the redeeming question has been omitted, and significantly Perceval is denied achievement of the Grail. Only the goody conformist Galahad, virtually perfect from the start, is granted success; and he then dies, unable to convey any benefit from his experience to the rest of humanity.

'The Book of Sir Launcelot and Queen Guinevere' is extracted from the very prolix 'prose Lancelot' which preceded the 'Quest'; and 'The Most Piteous Tale of the Morte Arthur' comes mainly from the psychological study at an all-too-human level which followed it, in which Arthur is a pathetically weak figure aged 92.

There is here, in fact, very little indeed that has anything at all to do with the Arthurian mysteries, as distinct from those of the Grail.

CHAPTER EIGHT

THE ARTHURIAN MYSTERIES

1. The Inworld Adventure

We are now in a position to consolidate and review the incidents identified in earlier sections which represent the successive stages on the Arthurian path of development, and to allow them to resonate further.

1 The mouth of the gleaming river.
The many references to the birth and childhood of Arthurian heroes—Culhwch, Taliesin, Gweir, Peredur, Merlin, Arthur himself—point to the experience which Wordsworth could still describe in the words 'Not in utter nakedness, but trailing clouds of glory do we come from God, who is our home. . .' First the astral body is drawn from the cauldron of Ceridwen, then the etheric body is gathered in the moon sphere, before the stream of earthly heredity is entered. The trial pieces from Tintagel establish that men still saw one another with an aura (Fig. 1), reminding them of this heavenly origin. It was still possible for the Arthurian initiate to go back through this gate in spirit-remembering, and to find what is called in *Owein* 'the loveliest vale in the world'. Alternatively this could be experienced as 'a light-form of indescribable beauty', or it might take the form of a maiden or of a white stag, enticing the hero to enter the forest of the otherworld.

2 New Moon, darkness.

Progress depends on forsaking the light of birth, which today no longer shines, and entering the darkness of death, the other gate out of ordinary daily consciousness. There, all sense-experiences cease (Peredur/Parzival cause the death of the Red Knight by a dart through the eye). More often this is expressed by the darkness of the forest, or by the barenness of the plain or wilderness. The kingdom may be barren because the king seized the golden cup of nourishment for himself. Self-centred desires for material aggrandizement and comfort, and materialistic thinking are, for spiritual experience, just such a dead wilderness which must be crossed. The starting-point for mankind today is the suppression of all desires of the senses in the process of meditation. Then the 'radiant brow' of the two-petal lotus begins to shine.

3 First Quarter. The Guardian of the Threshold.

The first figure to be met is the gatekeeper, usually Glewlwyd, 'Severe Grey One of the Mighty Dominion'. Care is taken to point out that he is no ordinary porter, but that on special occasions such as 'New Year' he controls entrance to the castle, to experience of *inner* spiritual processes. Gurnemans/Peredur's uncle effectively prevents Parzival/Peredur from reaching his goal whilst still unripe, by telling him not to ask questions. Sometimes a second Guardian is described, such as Custennin in *Culhwch* or the yellow-haired man in *Owein*. He stands on the path leading *outwards* as an idealized figure, against whom the individual can measure in what respect he falls short as a result of misdeeds in successive incarnations—his 'spiritual lineage'. This is the only way in which the pupil can 'push forward over the wall'.

4 Full Moon. Know Thyself.

This is a sunlit experience, but only in reflection, not directly. Culhwch meets Olwen, his higher self, the object of his striving; but she only tells him all that he must do before he may have her, namely, to put aside all wishes and accept his destiny as prescribed by the Giant, i.e., to 'know thyself'. The 'chief maiden' comes to Peredur by night, but he remains chaste; Parzival indeed marries Kondwiramurs, but must then endure long separation and travail before he sees her again. The cauldron will not boil the food of a coward.

At this stage the strength with which to achieve the aim is also given. Culhwch gains the support of Goreu, 'the best', whom we saw as representing the impulse of Jesus Christ. Parzival sees the Grail, also expressing the forces of Christ. The 'Book of the Holy Grail' appears. But this is only a first promise of what must gradually, through much effort, be brought to full effectiveness through the twelve-petal lotus.

5 Last Quarter. The Three Monsters.

The many monsters and giants in the legends can be fundamentally classified into three; and although these appear united in Giant Hawthorn or 'the horrors', they actually have to be tackled separately. In his head, man carried fixed ideas and preconceptions based on the senses, which lead to error and doubt of the spirit; these have to be replaced by a living, mobile thinking—the burnished sword—which can also grasp spiritual matters. In the breast, man carries likes and dislikes, selfishness, and criticism of those who follow the spiritual path; these need to be replaced by interest, the real experience of what the other person is feeling, and compassion. Man's limbs are hesitant to carry out what he knows to be right and good; fear of acting, the dragon in the will, must give way to courage and freewill. The spears of Giant Hawthorn must be grasped and thrown back at him, a turning of the will is called for.

6 Shallow, fleeting Mercury.

The shallow river has its surface constantly broken by eddies and whirlpools, light is everywhere flashing up and vanishing. Such are the two-dimensional Imaginative pictures of the elemental world, which at first light up in the soul somewhat chaotically; one cannot be sure whether their origin is objective or subjective. But as meditation progresses, real Imaginations—

the creamy horses used to the saddle, or the 'marvels'—appear, more intense and saturated than outer phenomena. The sixteen-petal lotus begins to be active. The blissful attraction of flower-filled meadows watered by a spring tempts one to linger, amid trees which continuously bear sweet-scented flowers and fruits. Peredur is entranced by the Imagination of his beloved occasioned by the black raven, the white snow and the red blood. This is the isle of Avalon.

7 *The Wood of Celidon (Venus)*

It is necessary to leave the lovely meadow and enter the special darkness of the forest of Celidon. The tree is stripped of every leaf by the hailstorm, all Imaginations so laboriously acquired have to be suppressed by further effort. This is a perilous passage, pictured by the battle with the black knight, the crossing of a torrent by a narrow plank, or the darkening of the sun. Cei and Cynon are forced to turn back, thinking can carry us no further. Gwalchmei and Owein, who have developed strongly active soul forces of the heart, press on. A new world of Inspiration begins to manifest as sound and rhythm out of the silence—bird-song, paeons of praise and the sounding of bells, or the rumbling of the black knight in the valley. Taliesin hears the sweet muse of poetry, Myrddin receives from Venus the Inspiration of his poems and prophecies.

8 *The Castle of the Sun.*

This is White Castle (Chapter 4.1), the castle of maidens, the revolving castle. It is the realm of selfless love, of Luned and the Lady of the Fountain, of Angharad Golden Hand, and of the Lady of the Bridle. It was in pre-Christian times the abode of the being known as Hu, later known as Christ. (Here Arthur carried the cross of Christ on his shield.) Here Owein and Gwalchmei in separate tales acquire the forces of the lion. It is marked in *Culhwch* by the contest between the radiant Gwythyr and the heartless Gwyn, summer and winter.

This completes the seven stages of purification of soul life, and is 'the island of the radiant door' that leads to spiritland.

Here the paths of the Arthurian initiation and of the Grail initiation diverge, the Grail path leading to the Castle of Marvels, the creative forces within man, whilst the Arthurian path continues further out into the cosmos.

9 The City of the Legion (Mars).

We are no longer in nature but in a city, and one occasioned by war. In *Gereint* the first encounter is with a single, very large knight, filled with pride; then comes a series of many encounters culminating in that with the Little King; this leads to the theme of 'death and resurrection'. In *Culhwch* we have on the one hand a series of skirmishes culminating in the killing of White Tusk Chief Boar, whose tusk is to be the sharp razor; on the other hand the winning of the rounded cauldron of Diwrnach, with the 'treasures of Ireland', representing the wisdom of the past. Peredur faces the Black Oppressor, and learns of the Worm of the Barrow, respectively, and needs the experience of balance indicated by the sheep that change colour as they cross the river, and the tree half green and half aflame. In modern spiritual science, Christ is experienced at the point of balance between the Powers named Lucifer and Ahriman.

10 On the Bank of Three Streams.

We come in *Culhwch* to the climax, the great 'battle' between Arthur and Twrch Trwyth, who was undergoing his kingship training and thus becoming a 'boar'. After inverting the images, we found him first acquiring the faculties of razor, shears and comb between the ears; then working with the seven piglets, the forces of the planetary spheres; and finally undergoing a contest with Arthur for nine nights and days, the period of the Odin initiation. Peredur frees the three sons killed daily by the Addanc of everyday consciousness who were restored overnight from their ordeal. But there is no refuge from the wind when it rages—the spiritual impulses originating from the Trinity will overwhelm man unless he has developed the inner strength to withstand them.

11 Mount Agned.
We have reached 'the uplands of Hell', the source of evil which is the necessary astral counterpart of physical creation—the Black Witch is actually the daughter of the White Witch. Peredur slays the Worm, which contains a precious stone; and he gives this to his man, he has achieved selflessness. Inverting the division of the Witch into two tubs, we perceive the counterpart of the deed of Marduk in dividing Tiamaat into heaven and earth, namely, the stage of consciousness called 'the union of the microcosm with the macrocosm'.

12 Mount Breguoin/Badon.
Peredur reaches the 'land of the revolving windmills', the lotus flowers, and rules for fourteen years. Arthur masters his '960 men', although his 'prowess beyond the glass fort' is not disclosed. Goreu inherits the property of the Giant, who voluntarily yields up his life, and Culhwch has Olwen at last.

2. Tintagel Revisited

Britain, and particularly the west coast of Cornwall, receives from the broad sweep of the Atlantic not only a prevailing wind which carries the element of salt far inland, but also the nurturing mildness of climate due to the Gulf Stream. Our etheric bodies were thus moulded by beings who were experienced, especially by the Celts who were awake to etheric forces, as the Genii of the Sea.[1] They spoke in an intensely living manner in the salt element, which crystallizes so readily, and worked directly into the nervous system and senses, making the British characteristically into observers, natural scientists. The quality of thinking could be developed strongly here— Arthur could, as a youth, 'draw the sword from the stone'.

We begin this visit in Rocky Valley at the carved finger-maze of the classical labyrinth (Plate 4), not far from where the stream enters the sea. We saw that this pattern has been used in Britain to induce a condition of trance and atavistic clairvoyance, and in India as a threshold mark and birth charm. It would not, therefore, be surprising if its original purpose was to enhance the experience of life before birth. If we enter the pattern meditatively, ascribing the seven rings to the courses of the planets, we can feel how the earthly form of man, the central incised cross, is condensed out of the planetary circles—the head receives its arched form from the spheres above, the lower limb-metabolic system is open to forces rising vertically from the earth, and the central rhythmic system of heart and lung is stimulated from the periphery in a twofold way, both directly (into the blood) and via the surrounding world (through the breath). We can thus say that one use of the finger-maze is likely to have been for instruction in the first 'battle' at the mouth of the gleaming river (Chapter 3.1). Incidentally, it is easy to see this design as the forerunner of the Celtic cross, the seven planetary rings being amalgamated into the single sun-ring when the Sun Spirit descended to earth.

The second 'battle' was characterized by the wilderness, the forest, or wherever sense-impressions were obliterated, in simulation of the stage of death. Such purely inner experience could be enhanced on the open moors, no longer used for astronomical observations, which may explain the structure there known as 'King Arthur's Hall'. But it could also be enhanced on the sea, as several legends connected with Manannan suggest. That this also occurred in Britain is shown by a lament in Welsh[2] connected with Tristan, which begins:

> Though I love the sea-shore I hate the sea
> That its wave should cover the rock of the hero,
> Brave, constant, courteous, generous, a strong support...
> The dispenser of fame has done an ill-omened favour—
> Till judgment day grief for it will endure...

We may certainly think of St Nectan's Kieve as a cult site, a 'divine grove', conveniently secluded from profane eyes, and with an atmosphere of enclosure eminently suited to stimulating experiences of the inner life of soul. Before the modern steps were constructed, the only approach would have been alongside the stream, and just before the present path begins to climb there is a small flat patch of rock convenient for guarding it. We have seen two pieces of evidence, from Tempe (Chapter 2.4) and from St Sampson's biographer (Chapter 6.1), that dramatic performances were given, and the natural ampitheatre at the foot of the Kieve may have been used to portray one or more of the third, fourth and fifth battles in this relatively dark and sombre area. The platform to the left of the fall would be well suited to more formal ceremonial. It is also conceivable that a pupil might have been required as a test of courage to dive from the platform into the basin. We can imagine what a strange experience it would be to emerge thence through the hole (Plate 3), partially supported by water behind only—one which could only be compared with that of birth.

We described in Chapter 3.6 how experiences of the elements were typified by the headland (earth), the cave (water), the Kieve (air), and the area of the carvings (fire), with a centre at Bossiney mound (the quintessence). Between that stage and the stage of Celidon wood (Chapter 3.7) were descriptions of some kind of a 'perilous passage', such as a test of the kind just mentioned might have provided. The stage of Celidon wood itself could also have unfolded in this area, where instances of spiritual hearing have already been mentioned (Chapter 2.1).

There can be no doubt that the eighth battle, that of White Castle, which marks the transition to spiritland, was an experience undergone on the promontory. It is there that Rudolf Steiner pictured so vividly (Chapter 2.4) the interplay of the beings of sunlight with those of air and water, and (Chapter 4.1) the way the Knights of the Round Table experienced the sun spirit differently before and after the descent of Christ to earth. The openness to wide vistas of sky and sea plays an essential part in this, and explains the need for the earliest rectangular buildings on the summit to provide shelter, whether or not they also served either from astronomical observations of the kind conducted on Bodmin moor, or simply as a lookout.

In the first lecture course Steiner gave in London[3] he spoke of the conflict with the two adversary powers, Lucifer and Ahriman (Chapter 4.2), who live not only in every human soul but also in the wind and cloud formations, and in the phenomena of tides, earthquakes and volcanic eruptions respectively. The promontory is not only obviously very exposed to the vagaries of our weather, but is actually composed of volcanic strata (Chapter 1.1). It is also rich in iron, the instrument of the Being called Michael,[4] who enables man to hold the balance against these two opposing powers.

At these higher stages we must recall Rudolf Steiner's remark that the help of twelve assistants, represented by the Round Table, was necessary. For this purpose we may think of a hall of the Round Table near the medieval castle ruins, which the thirteenth-century *Perceval li Gallois*[5] described as being 'next to the enclosure where the abysm is'.

The fact that the 'tunnel' (Plate 1) is cut with a sloping base means that the upper and lower entrances have a 'male' and a 'female' feeling. Steiner has described in detail[6] ceremonies of the Hibernian mysteries relating to a male and a female statue. These mysteries, for which the Irish twin-chambered 'horned cairns' were constructed, led to an exceptionally deep experience of the origin of the world and of man; and there is the possibility that the tunnel served for some modified form of them (the height and space does not allow for more) in the later age of the Arthurian mysteries. Alternatively, the tunnel might have served as a dolmen, the purpose of which was to exclude the physical sunlight but to admit through the roof-stone the spiritual forces of light, which vary according to the constellation in which the sun stands, and thus indicate the progress of the seasons. Or again, bearing in mind that the Arthurian mysteries were earth mysteries, inner experiences of the forces of the earth itself are likely to have been enhanced when descending below its surface. Only exact clairvoyance of the calibre of that of Steiner can say which of these possibilities was actually the case.

3. Arthur and his Companions

There is no consistency in early sources as to the names of the knights of the Round Table; but three names keep recurring in a variety of contexts in these sources: Cei, Gwalchmei and Bedwyr. We may ask what they represent in the context of the path of initiation, and how they are related to Arthur himself.

Cei is also mentioned in six early Irish texts, where he bears the epithet 'of fair judgment'; he is said to have been the one who awarded the underground realm to the Tuatha de Danaan or, in other words, to have forced the awareness of cosmic spirituality down into the subconscious. When in *Culhwch* Cei protests against the lad's admission to court, Arthur rebukes him as 'fair Cei'. An obvious characteristic is the energy with which he jumps into every situation, whether it be a dangerous adventure or simply to criticize, but is unable to succeed beyond a certain point. We saw him lauded by Arthur before the Guardian of the Threshold (Chapter 3.3), but subsequently conducting a faulty moon-initiation in conjunction with Gwenhwyvar (Chapter 3.8). In the Romances he becomes, in the words of Chrestien, 'very slanderous, mean, cutting and insolent'. His name itself consists of a hard, cutting expletive. Finally, he is said in the thirteenth-century *Perceval li Gallois*,[6] to slay Lacheu, Arthur's own son, and claim Lacheu (Loholt)'s achievement as his own. In all these cases we can recognize the activity of the intellect, acting to suppress atavistic insight. 'A wound from his sword no physician might heal.'

There is a duality in Cei's nature. In *'The Dream of Rhonabwy'* in the *Mabinogion* men at the periphery of a crowd flock towards him to see 'the handsomest man in Arthur's kingdom', whilst at the centre they flee outwards to avoid his horse. Similarly in *Culhwch* we first hear that at his birth Cei's father said to his mother 'The heart of your son will always be cold, and there will be no heat in his hands; he will be stubborn; when he carries a burden it will not be seen; no one will stand water or fire as well as he; there will be no officer or servant like him.' But later we are told that when the rain was heaviest, what was in or near his hand would stay dry because of his great heat, and when the cold was hardest he would be kindling to light a fire. When it pleased him, he would be as tall as the tallest tree in the forest (like the will-o'-the-wisps in Goethe's fairy-tale when they ate the gold). For nine days his breath lasted under water, and he could go without sleep for a similar time (in Ireland a chief poet had to keep himself in a trance for nine days). His full name, Cei mab Cynyr, is interpreted as 'Path son of Way'. We see pictured here the fact that the intellect can be burnished (Chapter 3.6) until the cold critical aspect is transformed into fiery spiritual concepts and Imaginations, representing a crucial step on the spiritual path.

Gwalchmei mab Gwyar, Hawk of the Plains son of Blood, is able to go further than Cei (his name constantly varies—Ualcmoe, Walwen, Gualganus, Gauvain, Gawan). He is a courteous lover, even fighting as champion of a little girl, and 'knew the material and essence of everything'. He achieves by loving words what others have failed to achieve by force—not only in *Parzival* and *Gereint* but in the Tristan fragment (Chapter 5.2).

In *Culhwch* Gwalchmei is the best walker and rider, who never came home without the quest he had gone to seek; but he plays little part. Geoffrey casts him as a nephew of Arthur. And in Malory he is still 'the man Arthur loved most'.

It is in the Romances that as Gawain he appears as representative of the sun-forces in the heart. His strength waxes and wanes as the day advances. In *The Mule without a Bridle* (Chapter 7.3) he enters the revolving castle of the sun, and, as in *Gawain and the Green Knight*,[8] plays the beheading game representing the loss of the head at the sun-stage after death; a game also played by Cuchulain with Cu Roi, another sun figure. In *Parzival* he is the leading Arthurian knight to follow the Grail quest, acquiring a Grail horse and reaching the Castle of Marvels as an alternate to Parzival. Here, as in the *Mule*, he conquers the lion, he masters the cosmic sun forces active in the heart. Again, he agrees for the sake of the reputation of Arthur's court to marry the 'Loathly Lady', and thus enables her to be beautiful either by day or by night; given the choice, he knows the secret of women and offers the choice to her, thus enabling her to be beautiful always.

The hawk had the reputation of reflecting the sun's rays before sunrise. Gwalchmei thus carries the sun-force of love, and the force of the Word, into the feelings of the heart; he is a true 'son of blood'.

Bedwyr (creativity) son of Bedrawc (fourfoldness) often accompanies Arthur, but little is said of him—he represents the strong, silent and unconscious will. In the poem quoted in Chapter 3.5 he was described as 'strong of sinew', and men fell before him 'a hundred at a time'. In *Culhwch* 'no one but Arthur was as fair as he. Though he were single-handed, no three warriors could draw blood sooner than he', for the will works directly into the blood. And the head of his spear will draw blood from the wind and settle upon the shaft again— he draws strength from the spirit. He was the first to catch and throw back a spear cast by the Giant, striking him in the kneecap, the sensitive spot of the limb system. And he participates in the freeing of Mabon and the killing of Dillus. He plays little part in the Romances, but according to Malory it is Sir Bedivere who is thrice commanded to throw Excalibur, representing Arthur's life-forces, into the mystic lake, and who carries his body to its shore to meet the ship that bears it to Avalon. Man's will carries his impulses into the future. Bedwyr is the only person other than Arthur to extend a Triad as a fourth person. Triad 21 lists as the three 'battle-diademed men' Drystan son of Tallwch, Hueil son of Caw and Cei son of Cenyr; 'and one was diademed above the three of them: that was Bedwyr son of Bedrawc'. This may have something to do with his 'fourfoldness'. Steiner is reported[10] to have said in conversation that Bedwyr was regarded as also a representative of the ego, the fourth principle of man; Trystan, even more than Gwalchmei the archetypal lover, as representing the astral body; Cei the etheric body, in which thinking is rooted; and Hueil the physical body.

Hueil is depicted in Caradoc's *Life of Gildas*[11] (c.1100). Hueil and Gildas are among the twenty-four sons of Cawr (giant). 'Hueil, an active warrior and most distinguished soldier, submitted to no king, not even to Arthur, but with his brothers constantly rose against him. . . He used to harass the latter and provoke the greatest anger between them. He would often sweep down from Scotland, set up conflagrations, and carry off spoils with victory and renown. Arthur pursued the victorious and excellent youth who, as the inhabitants used to assert and hope, was destined to become king. In the hostile pursuit and council of war in the Isle of Man he killed the young plunderer, and returned rejoicing that he had overcome his bravest enemy.' This is a very fair picture of the efforts made in the mysteries to free oneself from the physical body and the impressions of the senses (Chapter 3.2). But many 'inhabitants' regard this body as 'king'.

In this context we may regard Arthur as representing the Higher Self of man, which is freed from the physical and directs the activity of the three soul forces of thinking, feeling and willing—Cei, Gwalchmei and Bedwyr—in the soul-spiritual world, where in the absence of the physical body they need to be co-ordinated.

Why then, we may ask, was the name 'Arthur' chosen for the leader of this mystery school over many centuries? The name would be pre-Celtic in origin, and only later Romanized as 'Arturus', rather than the other way round, as commonly supposed. (The connection with Arcturus, Ursa Major, and the far north seems to be a twelfth-century variant.) Rhys pointed out[12] last century that the syllable 'Art' is related to the Gaulish goddess Artio, German Erta/Nerthus, English 'Earth'; and that this Brythonic stem led to a group of words in Cornish and Welsh around 'ardu', to plough—we saw an example of this in Chapter 6.2. The sounds themselves confirm it, combined with the natural expression for reverence and devotion to the divine, 'Ah' is combined with the downward-pointing 't' or 'd' which carry the divine impulse down into the earth— we are dealing with cosmic-earthly mysteries. (Triad 20 asserts that 'no grass or plants used to spring up for seven years where Arthur walked'.) The second syllable is likely to derive from the name of the sun-god, Hu, the pre-Christian name of Christ (Chapter 4.1). Hu, meaning 'yoke', is said to have introduced to Britain the use of the plough. The suffix 'r' may be purely euphonious, or may perhaps be a relic of the name for the higher forces of life flowing from the sun, known in Egypt as Ra and in Ireland as Roi.

The name 'Arthur' thus expresses accurately the connection between sun and earth which we saw (Chapter 2.4) as the central experience of the Arthurian knights in the weaving sunlight and nature forces at Tintagel.

4. The Destiny of Arthur

Around 2400 BC, when the power known in Christian-Hebrew terminology as Michael was ruling human evolution, careful observations of the heavens were being made on Bodmin Moor. These astronomer-priests were not only aware of the points of light which we see, but still had clairvoyant vision of the activities of the spiritual beings of the Hierarchies, whose bodily presence the light of the stars makes manifest. But this vision steadily faded, and became increasingly difficult to attain. It became clear that a new way must be found to carry as much as possible of the accumulated star-wisdom into the centuries of spiritual darkness that were foreseen, and a new Mystery Centre was to be founded for this purpose. In the place of clear starry (astral) vision, experience of the elemental (etheric) world must increasingly be relied upon.[13]

Tintagel was chosen as the site because it combined a fine panorama displaying the interplay of sunlight, warmth and air with sea and rock, a diversity of watery (etheric) experiences within a narrow compass, and youthful earth forces combined with the presence of iron, the earthly instrument of Michael. It also had the physical advantages of easy defensibility, fresh water, and a central situation on the highway of the Irish Channel, yet somewhat apart from the main traffic of the Camel estuary. The Hibernian priest responsible for its inauguration came to be known as Merlin.

Around 1200 BC a new age was being heralded by the spread of the proto-Celts, the Urnfielders, across Europe from the east. They were specially sensitive to the etheric world, and the new Mystery was entrusted to their care and nurturing. But each leader who was to fill the rank of Arthur had to undergo initiation in both the Hibernian mysteries and the Northern mysteries of Wotan and Sig, which bore the tragic tone of 'The Twilight of the Gods'.

It was widely understood that twelve different spiritual forces flow from the regions of the zodiac, but to take hold of these forces had now become beyond the power of a single individual. A group of men was therefore necessary, who together formed a kind of organism through which a higher Being could work, as the human soul works through the several organs of the body. Arthur therefore gathered around him twelve individuals, who regarded themselves as representing the twelve attributes of the Godhead, a zodiacal symbol displayed above each of them indicating the particular cosmic influence with which he was associated. The thirteenth represented the 'Holy Three', as the *Edda* expresses it, the Trinity; he was the link enabling the higher Being to descend into its organism. Whoever filled the rank of Arthur was the purely spiritual monarch of this group of twelve Celtic initiate-priests, who came to be known as the Knights of the Round Table, the great White Lodge of the West.

The twelve did not claim personal intelligence, but felt that their intelligence was revealed by the Power known as Michael—the Chaldean Marduk and perhaps the Welsh Myrddin—who still administered the cosmic intelligence; and after 2160 years he was again ruling human evolution around 300 BC, when these mysteries were to reach their peak. They were thus essentially a Michael community.

The diverse and subtle experiences they attained of the interplay between sunlight and planetary influences as these passed through the zodiac in the course of the year, and of the ever-changing interplay of light and air, water and rock, poured into their hearts and all through their etheric bodies, into their very being. Thunder and lightning, rain or sunshine, the course and movement of the stars, the rise or set of sun or moon, were all seen as quite definite gestures of divine spiritual Beings, in the same way that we interpret gestures of hand or eyelid as expressing the intention of a human being. Forces from the interior of the earth were equally studied in some detail. In this way the elemental beings—no longer the angelic hierarchies—brought them messages from the whole cosmos. They felt it all as a reflection of their own incessant inner battles, where their enlightened ego-consciousness strove to master the fog of their passions.

It was necessary that a firm foundation should be given in the West for the development of the ego, by educating a human race with strong physical forces into which it could be entrenched. The basis for this was supplied by the hardy, robust forces indwelling the barbaric peoples of north-west Europe. The initiates drew the strength they needed to cultivate and civilize these peoples from Christ, whom they received into themselves—although not under that name—even before His descent to earth. The priesthood became a knighthood. Their battles with the wild savagery which still dominated the astral bodies of large masses of these barbarian peoples are pictured in the legends as 'Adventure', the overcoming of monsters, giants and other perils. Everything was done in such a way that each individual knew and realized his connection with the other knights.

Just as the Chaldean Magi could, through their star-knowledge, foresee the coming of Christ, so too could the initiates of the Hibernian and Arthurian mysteries. Hence the Mystery of Golgotha was taken up with enthusiasm, and led over without conflict into the growth of Celtic Christianity, whose missionaries continued to follow the tracks of the

Arthurian knights into Europe. If this stream could have been pursued, souls would inevitably have experienced union with the spiritual world. The developing feeling of the independent ego inevitably encountered, however, all that flowed from the narration of the events in Palestine. Roman language and culture was spreading like a dark cloud over Europe, cutting men off from what remained of direct experience of the spirit—as, for example, in the extermination of the druids in Anglesey—and substituting the cult. Into the spiritual life was thrust dogmatically the abstract Roman legal system, whose proper sphere was that of politics and human rights. Spirituality was thereby dragged down into the human world, with no upward glance into the supersensible. The battle of the Arthurian mysteries against this was misinterpreted by Geoffrey as the physical battle against Rome. The outcome was determined not by the superiority of Rome, but by 'treachery' at home, namely the failure within the Arthurian mysteries themselves to recognize that Christ had actually left the sun, and that intelligence no longer came from angels under the rulership of Michael, but had become the property of individual men. The knights were indeed battling for the real Christ impulse, but would not abandon their conviction that the sun was still the fount of Christianity, even though they had perceived the change as it poured into the forces of the earth. Hence they continued to work longer than any other community to ensure that Michael retained his ancient dominion over the intelligence.

Meanwhile a high individuality, long concerned with the spiritual activities of the Round Table, had taken into his keeping the vessel in which was collected the blood on Golgotha, and had withdrawn into higher worlds. Centuries later he incorporated in the figure known as Titurel, and founded a new mystery centre, each pupil of which could bear the name of Parzival. In the ninth century, whilst a few people were still able to understand Christianity in astral vision, the Arthurian stream of Cosmic Christianity came together with the Grail stream moving in the hearts and souls of men. Parzival experienced out of his individual capacity the twelvefoldness of the zodiac, and also achieved the Grail—but not without taking with him his brother from the East. Even in the eleventh century there still hovered over the school of Chartres something of the sun-Christianity which had belonged to the Arthurian stream.

Early in the thirteenth century the ancient esotericism flickered out. Through its mingling with the mood of cult and ritual there arose in its place the world of chivalry, with the picture of physical humanity on earth at its centre. But something of the Celtic love of democracy flowed into political life. In Wales the Arthurian centre continued, but the knights no longer stood on the old level; for the age of love had become the age of egoism, where men sought to master lands through the sword. The Round Table became merely secular, a source of entertainments. In England, after the birth of a prince named Arthur to Henry VII, an Order of Arthur was founded for purely political ends. The Round Table was finally abolished in the reign of Queen Elizabeth I, for political reasons. Various occult societies continued to echo its traditions; but the esoteric secrets had 'disappeared into the Atlantic Ocean'.

Only the Arthurian legends remained. Since the seventh century minstrels had wandered through Europe, and during the tenth and eleventh centuries the substance which we have been examining was added to their repertoire. They recreated pictures and thought-forms composed by those who gave ear to others able to impart spiritual seeds which remained alive in men's souls, and which would grow in our own time into a different kind of understanding for the spirit.

5. Arthur's Return

We know that in 1113 a belief existed in Cornwall that 'Arthur' was not dead but recuperating somewhere, and that his return was awaited, because a riot broke out in Bodmin when visiting

French priests dared to question it. But Geoffrey of Monmouth, who used a Cornish source, remained silent about the question of Arthur's death in deference to his ecclesiastical masters. There is no trace of such a belief in the earliest Welsh sources, although according to the *Stanzas of the Graves* 'a grave for Arthur is not known'. But we have William of Malmesbury's assurance in 1125 that the belief was also widespread in Brittany, where it was adopted by Wace in 1155.

What was actually meant by such an idea? The concept of reincarnation was widely understood in Britain before it was suppressed by Rome—classical authors make this clear, and we have found examples in *Preiddu Annwn* (Chapter 2.5), *Owein* (Chapter 5.1) and Elis Gryffyd (Chapter 5.3). There would therefore have been originally no point in singling out Arthur in this connection. There was later an obvious political implication that before long Britain would be freed from foreign yoke, an implication seized on by both Henry I and Henry VII in naming their eldest son Arthur—in both cases to no avail. But the thesis of this study has been that 'Arthur' was a rank, the leader of a mystery school which existed at Tintagel for many centuries prior to the fifth century AD. In this sense, the 'return of Arthur' would point to the renewal of a spiritual impulse such as was remembered by the Cornish as having once existed at Tintagel, leading to a culture once again based on spiritual-moral values.

Around AD 1900 the five thousand years predicted by Indian esotericism for Kali Yuga, the Dark Age (Chapter 2.2) had run its course. Two decades earlier the Archangel Michael, who led human evolution at the time when the cairns and circles were built on Bodmin Moor, and again in the centuries immediately before Christ when the Arthurian mystery was at its peak (Chapter 8.4), once again entered on his earthly task. A new age of light had begun. And as one of the last mystery centres to cease activity, the Arthurian mystery needs to be among the first to be re-established. Out of this could then be recovered the content which it was their task to preserve from the older Hibernian and Northern mysteries. At a time when older moral values are fast vanishing, the future moral-spiritual life of Britain seems intimately connected with the task of reawakening such an impulse as a gift to the world as a whole.

Welsh folk-lore from various places, including Snowdon, recounts that Arthur, like Barbarossa and Charlemagne, lies sleeping with his warriors in a cave deep within the mountain. Whereas in Tintagel the knights had observed the elemental beings active in light and air, in such a cave could be experienced the earth forces working up both into the plants and into man's own being. By this is meant not only physical forces like gravity, electricity or nuclear energy now known to science, but also their moral aspects. The mysteries of Arthur were mysteries of the earth, of agricultural festivals and the round of economic life. And as the knights experienced Christ in the elements of outer nature from above and from below, so today we need to learn to recognize Christ as the bringer of balance and healing between the forces from above and below the earth's surface, known as Lucifer and Ahriman (Chapter 4.2), preparatory to being able to behold Him.

The legends of Arthur's death developed from Breton sources by Wace describe how, after the mortal wound at Camblan, Arthur's sword Excalibur is thrown into a lake, where it is grasped by a mysterious hand rising from the water. We saw (Chapter 3.6) the particular connection of the Arthurian mysteries with water. The lake is the elemental world, into which thoughts ordinarily dissolve at death, but through the experiences of that world by the Round Table, the burnished sword of thinking could be caught hold of and carried further. The dead mineral which can be weighed, counted and grasped in the rigid concepts of modern science is only the corpse of what was once living, and to grasp this effectively thought must be further transformed to Imaginations which unite in love with the surrounding world. The most recent science must increasingly take account of imponderables. The Green Movement is already feeling its way towards understanding the earth as a living organism, but needs support from the inner schooling of thinking which a renewal of the mysteries can bring.

Layamon (Chapter 7.2) then tells how Arthur himself was carried to the lake, and met by maidens in a mysterious boat. According to a late Welsh source they were led by Barynthus through the planetary spheres to the palace of Morgan-la-Faye, the 'sea-born fairy', that one of the nine sisters who knew the healing arts, and 'of astronomy could she enough, for Merlin had her taught'. The spiritual substance of the Arthurian mystery, its task ended with the emergence of the Grail mystery, was withdrawn into the supersensible world of the nine priestesses, the nine divine Hierarchies. Today it has again become possible to enter not only into a mathematical relationship to the stars, but also into a feeling and spiritual relationship, and thus to begin to renew the Arthurian heritage transmitted from earlier ages.

The most important content of the Arthurian mysteries, which steps were taken to preserve at the time of their decline, was the path of self-development leading the soul out to spiritual experience of the cosmos, which has been surveyed in Chapter 8.1. It led by way of purification of the soul, the confrontation with the Guardian of the Threshold, the demands of the threefold Giant, and the realm of the elements, to the planetary spheres. We understood Nennius to be describing this as a necessary training for kingship. But we live in an age when such a path must be, and is, open not only to kings but to every human being who cares to undergo the discipline involved. Each individual thus rises to kingly stature as ruler of his own inner being.

The fruits of the mystery training were carried by the knights out into the civilization of the time, purifying the material desires of less disciplined souls and leading them towards a harmonious social life. To speak of the 'return of Arthur' implies that there will be added to the present civilization, based as it is on selfishness and material values, perhaps after crisis and collapse, a more advance civilization in which spiritual development (initiation) is once again valued decisively, and moral-spiritual values again predominate. The longing for such a change has already manifest in the so-called 'alternative society'. But it can only become reality when spiritual movements which genuinely serve man's progressive evolution succeed in placing freedom and love above the egoistic self-interest which keeps others in a situation of complacency, spiritual ignorance and dependence, whether through economic constrictions, political power or religious dogmatism. We need each to discover the reality of the spirit within us; we must each, in words ascribed to Taliesin, 'set Elphin free'.

Nature at Tintagel is still quick with spirit in the interplay between sunlit air and foaming waves. But each one of us must discover through his own inner activity the sources of the spirit, no longer limited to a special place, but wherever life itself may lead us. Thereby Michael can once again direct the evolution of humanity, but now in co-operation with us. And thereby, as foretold, Arthur at last truly reawakens from his long sleep.

BIBLIOGRAPHY

GA (Gesamtausgabe) refers to the volume number in the Complete Edition of the works of Rudolf Steiner in the original German.

PREFACE

1 *Studia Celtica X/XI*, 1975/6. R. Bromwich, *Concepts of Arthur.*
2 A. C. L. Brown, *Origin of the Grail Legend.* Cambridge, Mass., 1943.
3 R. Steiner, GA 227, *The Evolution of Consciousness.* London, 1966,
   GA9, *Theosophy.* London, 1973.

CHAPTER ONE—TINTAGEL AND ITS PROBLEMS

1 G. Ashe (ed), *The Quest for Arthur's Britain.* London, 1968.
2 C. A. Ralegh Radford, *Tintagel Castle, Cornwall.* London, 1935.
3 C. Thomas, *Tintagel Castle.* London, 1986.
4 L. Thorpe (tr). Geoffrey of Monmouth, *The History of the Kings of Britain.* Harmondsworth, 1966.
5 A. C. L. Brown, *Origin of the Grail Legend.*
6 M. Williams, *Tintagel to Boscastle.* Bodmin, 1975.
7 F. J. Snell, *King Arthur's Country.* London, 1926.
8 A. C. Canner, *The Parish of Tintagel.* Enfield, 1982.
9 C. O'Brien, *The Megalithic Odyssey.* Wellingborough, 1983.
10 F. Teichman, *Der Mensch und sein Tempel: Megalithkultur.* Stuttgart, 1983.
11 *Journal Royal Institute of Cornwall XII*, 1927. H. Jenner, *Tintagel Castle in History and Romance.*

12 *Eriu XII*, 1971. C. Thomas, *Rosnat, Rostat and the early Irish Church*.

13 R. Bromwich, *Trioedd Ynys Prydein*. Cardiff, 1961.

14 *Aberystwyth Studies VIII*, 1926. T. Gwynn-Jones, *Some Arthurian Material in Keltic*.

15 R. Hunt, *Popular Romances of the West of England*. London, 1871.

16 J. Armitage Robinson, *Two Glastonbury Legends*. Cambridge, 1926.

17 H. Newstead, *Bran the Blessed in Arthurian Romance*. Cambridge, 1939.

CHAPTER TWO—THE OTHERWORLD DIMENSION

1 W. Greiner, *Eleusis—Göttermythos und Einweihungsweg*. Dornach CH, 1982.

H. Ehrhardt, *Samothrake*. Stuttgart, 1985.

B. Wulf, *Athen und Ephesus*. Freiburg im Breisgau, 1978.

H. Gsänger, *Externsteine*. Schaffhausen CH, 1983.

2 R. Steiner, GA 144, 7 Feb. 1913, *The Mysteries of the East and of Christianity*. London, 1972.

3 G. Wachsmuth, *The Life and Work of Rudolf Steiner*. New York, 1955.

4 R. Steiner, GA 240, 21 & 27 Aug. 1924, *Karmic Relationships, Vol VIII*. London, 1975.

5 T. Darvil, *Prehistoric Britain*. London, 1987.

6 R. Steiner, GA 133, 20 May 1912, *Earthly and Cosmic Man*. New York, 1986.

7 R. Steiner, GA 243, 11-12 Aug. 1923, *True and False Paths in Spiritual Investigation*. London, 1986.

8 E. Davies, *Celtic Researches*. London, 1804.

9 R. Robins, *Circles of Silence*. London, 1985.

10 R. Steiner, GA 116, 25 Oct. 1909, *The Christ Impulse and the Development of Ego-Consciousness*. New York, 1976.

11 *Trans. Cymmrodorion* 1933/5. A. Dolmetsch, *Ancient Welsh Music*.

12 R. Graves, *The White Goddess*. London, 1961.

13 R. Steiner, GA 223, 31 Mar.-8Apr. 1923, *The Cycle of the Year*. New York, 1984.
    GA 219, 23 Dec. 1922, *Man and the World of the Stars*. New York, 1963.

14 R. Steiner, GA 232, 7-9 Dec. 1923, *Mystery Knowledge and Mystery Centres*. London, 1973.

15 K. Jackson, *Studies in Early Celtic Nature Poetry*. Cambridge, 1935.
16 E. Davies, *Mythology and Rites of the British Druids*. London, 1809.
17 R. Steiner, GA 119, 26 Mar. 1910, *Macrocosm and Microcosm*. London, 1986.
18 A. Burl, *The Stonehenge People*. London, 1987.
19 *Das Albert Steffen Buch*. Dornach CH, 1944. R. Steiner, verse, not translated.
20 *Studia Celtica 18/19*, 1983/4. M. Haycock, *Preiddeu Annwn and the Figure of Taliesin*.
21 D. W. Nash, *Taliesin*. London, 1858.
22 A. W. Wade-Evans, *Nennius's History of the Britons*. London, 1938.
23 *Nottingham Mediaeval Studies VIII*, 1964. T. Jones, *Early Evolution of the Legend of Arthur*.
24 *Modern Philology XLIII*, 1945/6. K. Jackson, *Once Again Arthur's Battles*.
25 A. B. Cook, *Zeus: A Study in Ancient Religion*. Cambridge, 1940.

CHAPTER THREE—BATTLES OF THE SOUL

1 A. and B. Rees, *Celtic Heritage*. London, 1961.
2 L. Thorpe (tr), Geoffrey of Monmouth. *The History of the Kings of Britain*.
3 R. Steiner, GA 124, 19 Dec. 1910, *Background to the Gospel of St Mark*. London, 1985.
4 Lady C. Guest, *The Mabinogion*. London, 1877.
   P. K. Ford, *The Mabinogi*. Berkeley, Cal., 1977.
5 R. Steiner, GA 34, *The Education of the Child*. London, 1975.
6 J. Williams ab Ithel (tr). Llwelyn Sion, *Barddas*. Llandovery, 1842.
7 K. H. Jackson in R. H. Loomis (ed) *Arthurian Literature in the Middle Ages*.
8 R. Steiner, GA 243, 12 Aug. 1924, *True and False Paths in Spiritual Investigation*.
9 R. Graves, *The White Goddess*.
10 R. Steiner, GA 9, *Theosophy*.
11 D. Wright (tr) *Beowulf*. Harmondsworth, 1957.
12 William of Malmesbury, *De Antiquitate Glastoniae*. c. 1125.
13 R. Steiner, GA 95, 24 Aug. 1906, *At the Gates of Spiritual Science*. London, 1986.
14 T. Dean and T. Shaw, *Folklore of Cornwall*. London, 1975.

15 R. Steiner, GA 153, 11 Apr. 1914, *The Inner Nature of Man*. Vancouver, 1959.
16 R. Bromwich, *Trioedd Ynys Prydein*.
17 *Modern Philology 17*, 1920. T. P. Cross, *A Welsh Tristan Episode*.
18 R. Steiner, GA 227, 19 Aug. 1923, *The Evolution of Consciousness*.
19 R. Steiner, GA 233, 13 Jan. 1924, *Rosicrucianism and Modern Initiation*. London, 1965.
20 H. Williams (tr), *Gildas*. Caradoc of Llancarvan. *Life of Gildas*. London, 1901.
21 *Speculum XIII*, 1937/8. M. Williams, *An Early Ritual Poem in Welsh*.

CHAPTER FOUR—TRIALS OF THE SPIRIT

1 W. Stokes, *Tripartite Life of St Patrick*, Pt II. London, 1887.
2 R. Steiner, GA 208, 6 Nov. 1921, *The Sun Mystery in the Course of Human History*. London, 1955.
3 St Augustine, *Confessions*, Book VII.
4 R. Steiner, GA 240, 21 Aug. 1924, *Karmic Relationships, Vol VIII*.
5 J. Williams ab Ithel (tr), Llwelyn Sion. *Barddas*.
6 R. Steiner, GA 57, 6 May. 1909, *Anthroposophical Quarterly 9/1*, 1964. *European Mysteries and their Initiates*.
7 R. Steiner, GA 191, 1-15 Nov. 1919, *Influences of Lucifer and Ahriman*. New York, 1976.
8 R. Steiner, GA 147, 30 Aug. 1913, *Secrets of the Threshold*. London, 1928.
9 R. Bromwich, *Trioedd Ynys Prydein*, Appx. III.
10 A. Wade-Evans, *Nennius's History of the Britons*.
11 R. Steiner, GA 10, *Knowledge of the Higher Worlds. How is it Achieved?* Part II. London, 1976.
12 R. Steiner, GA 327, 16 June 1924, *Agriculture*. London, 1958.
13 Y. *Cymmrodor*, 1918. J. Morris-Jones. *Taliesin*.

CHAPTER FIVE—OTHER BRITISH HEROES

1 R. Steiner, GA 231, 14 Nov. 1923, *Supersensible Man*. New York, 1961.
2 A. Hatto (tr), Gottfried of Strassbourg. *Tristan*. Harmondsworth, 1960.
3 Private manuscript by E. Wolfram after conversations with R. Steiner.

4 Lady C. Guest, *The Mabinogion*. London, 1906.
5 L. Thorpe (tr), Geoffrey of Monmouth. *History of the Kings of Britain*.
6 *Etudes Celtique VIII*, 1959. T. Jones, *Myrddin and Five Dreams of Gwendydd*.
7 *Univ. Illinois Studies in Language and Literature, 1925*. J. J. Parry, *Vita Merlini*.
8 N. Tolstoi, *The Quest for Merlin*. London, 1985.
9 R. J. Stewart, *The Prophetic Vision of Merlin*. London, 1986.
10 R. Steiner, GA 196, 18 Jan. 1920, *Golden Blade*, 1960. *Some Conditions for Understanding Supersensible Experiences*.
11 E. Davies, *The Mythology and Rites of the British Druids*.
12 R. Steiner, GA 240, 21 Aug. 1924, *Karmic Relationships, Vol VIII*.
13 E. C. Merry, *The Flaming Door*. Edinburgh, 1983.
14 R. Graves, *The White Goddess*.
15 D. W. Nash, *Taliesin*.

CHAPTER SIX—AFTER TINTAGEL

1 K. Jackson, *Language and History in Early Britain*. Edinburgh, 1953.
2 R. Bromwich, *Trioedd Ynys Prydein*.
3 R. Graves, *The White Goddess*.
4 See Chapter Four, reference 6.
5 R. Steiner, GA 121, 12 June 1910, *The Mission of the Individual Folk Souls*. London, 1970.
6 L. Hardinge, *The Celtic Church in Britain*. London, 1972.
7 J. Streit, *Sun and Cross*. Edinburgh, 1984.
8 R. S. Loomis, *Wales and the Arthurian Legend*. Cardiff, 1956.
9 G. Goetinck, *Peredur*. Cardiff, 1975.
10 J. D. Bruce, *Evolution of Arthurian Romance*. Göttingen and Baltimore, 1923.
11 W. Rath (tr), *Das Buch vom Gral*. Stuttgart, 1968.
12 R. Steiner, GA 240, 21 Aug. 1924, *Karmic Relationships Vol VIII*.
13 R. Steiner, GA 237, 13 Jul. 1924, *Karmic Relationships, Vol III*. London, 1977.
14 R. Steiner, GA 15, 1911, *The Spiritual Guidance of Mankind*. New York, 1976.

CHAPTER SEVEN—CHRONICLERS AND ROMANCERS

1 L. Thorpe (tr), Geoffrey of Monmouth. *History of the Kings of Britain.*
2 *Trans. Soc. Cymmrodorion, 1912/3.* W. J. Gruffyd, *The Mabinogion.*
3 E. Mason (tr), Wace and Layamon. *Arthurian Chronicles.* London, 1912.
4 *Studies and Notes in Philology,* 7. A. C. L. Brown, *The Round Table before Wace.*
5 W. W. Comfort (tr), Chrestien de Troyes. *Arthurian Romances.* London, 1914.
6 E. Brewer (tr), *From Cuchulain to Gawain.* Cambridge, 1973.
7 G. Goetinck, *Peredur.*
8 R. Steiner, GA 97, 29 Jul. 1906, Not published in English.
9 N. Bryant (tr), Chrestien de Troyes. *Perceval.* Woodbridge, 1982.
10 H. M. Mustard & C. E. Passage (tr), Wolfram von Eschenbach. *Parzival.* New York, 1961.
11 W. J. Stein, *The Ninth Century and the Holy Grail.* London, 1988.
12 H. Teutschmann, *Der Gral—Weisheit und Liebe.* Dornach CH, 1984.
13 E. Vinaver, *The Works of Thomas Malory.* London, 1954.

CHAPTER EIGHT—THE ARTHURIAN MYSTERIES

1 R. Steiner, GA 158, 15 Nov. 1914, Not Published in English.
2 *Studia Celtica xiv/v,* 1979/80. R. Bromwich, *A Tristan Poem.*
3 R. Steiner, GA 218, 16 Nov. 1922, *The Planetary Spheres and their Influence.* London, 1982.
4 R. Steiner, GA 229, 5 Oct. 1923, *The Four Seasons and the Archangels.* London, 1984.
5 S. Evans (tr), *The High History of the Holy Grail (Perlesvaus).* London, 1910.
   I. Wyatt, *From Round Table to Grail Castle.* East Grinstead, 1979.
6 R. Steiner, GA 232, 7-9 Dec. 1923, *Mystery Knowledge and Mystery Centres.*
7 Lady C. Guest (tr), *The Mabinogion,* Note.
8 B. Stone (tr), *Sir Gawain and the Green Knight.* Harmondsworth, 1959.
9 J. L. Weston, *Reliques of Ancient Poetry.*

10 See Chapter Five, reference 3.

11 H. Williams (tr), *Gildas*. Caradoc of Llancarvan. *Life of Gildas*.

12 J. Rhys, *Studies in Arthurian Legend*. Oxford, 1891.

13 This section draws on remarks by R. Steiner in various lectures, mainly unpublished in English.

CHRONOLOGICAL LIST
(All dates are approximate)

3000 BC   Age of Sentient Soul begins in Egypt, Chaldea, British Isles.

2400   Michael Regency (300 yrs). Circles and cairns on Bodmin Moor

1500   Rocky Valley carvings, tumuli. Titans banished from Greece to Britain

1280   Moses leaves Egypt. Egyptian wisdom of cosmos carried west.

1100   Arthurian Mystery Centre founded at Tintagel. Proto-Celts arrive.

750   Age of Intellectual Soul begins in Greece.

600   Pythagoras taught by Abaris from Hyperborea. True Celts arrive.

550   Michael Regency begins. Arthurian Mysteries reach their peak.

200   Barras Head and Willapark fortified.

33 AD   Mystery of Golgotha. Change in Sun-working recognized at Tintagel.

59   Romans exterminate druids in Anglesey.

175   Welsh King Lucius baptised in Rome.

203   Tertullian writes on non-Roman Christians in Britain.

250, 320   Two Roman-British milestones erected near Tintagel.

350   Stone buildings on Tintagel crest.

397   Abbey of Whithorn founded. Pelagius preaching in Rome.

400	Cunedda evicts Irish from Gwynedd. Irish incursions in Cornwall.
411	Last Romans leave. Churches being founded, e.g. Welsh Bicknor.
418	Death of Pelagius.
430	Mission of Germanus to Britain and Ireland (not Cornwall).
432	Patrick to Ireland, finds many Christians already.
450	Century of migration of Celtic Saints.
480	'Historical' Arthur born? Fresh incursion of Irish in Cornwall.
500	Second long stone building at Tintagel. St Juliot near Camelford.
519	Battle of Badon? Illtuyd founds monasteries at Caldey and Llantwit.
535	Columba unites Celtic and Roman churches in Ireland.
537	Dyfrig (Dubricius) retires.
539	Camlan, death of 'historical' Arthur?.
550	David converts Wales. Gildas writes. Sampson passes through Cornwall.
570	Aneurin, Taliesin, Llewarch Hen writing. Extension of Tintagel.
573	Arfderydd overrun, 'historical' Merlin flees to forest of Celidon.
575	Saxons reach the Wye. Columba defends the Bards.
597	Augustine reaches England.
600	Battle of Gododdin.
664	England attached to Rome (Synod of Whitby).
715	*Beowulf* written. Wales submits to Rome.
750	*The Book of the Grail.* Irish legends written down. Boniface defeats druids in Germany.
800	Charlemagne (d.814). Vikings attacking Britain and Ireland.
830	Nennius writing.
850	Cornwall submits to Canterbury. *Culhwch and Olwen* composed orally. *Heliand* and *Edda* written. Scotus Erigena active.
879	'Historical' Parzival. Meeting of Arthur and Grail streams.

900	*Annales Cambriae* end. Death of Alfred.
945	Transfer of Cymry from North to South Wales. Laws of Hwel Dda.
950	*Fruits of the Inworld* and other pseudo-Taliesin poems written.
965	Invasion of Gwynedd.
1040	Congress of Welsh and Irish musicians records traditional music.
1050	Four Branches of *Mabinogion* written.
1066	Norman Conquest.
1100	*Culhwch and Olwen* written down. Bleddri active. Arthur portrayed at Modena.
1125	William of Malmesbury's *Guesta*. Templars recognized by Rome.
1136	Geoffrey of Monmouth's *Historia*.
1140/75	Reginald builds at Tintagel.
1150	*Who is Guardian*. Wace writing.
1160	Beroul and Thomas write *Tristans*.
1165	Marie de France. Oxford University founded. Council against Albigenses.
1170	Chrestien's *Lancelot, Perceval*. Murder of Becket.
1175	*Black Book of Carmarthen* written down.
1188	Gerald of Wales.
1195	Layamon's *Brut*. *Elder Edda*.
1200	Robert de Boron's metrical *Joseph*. *Rhonabwy*. *Niebelungenlied*.
1205	Wolfram's *Parzival*.
1210	Gottfried's *Tristan*. Albigensian Crusade.
1225	Oldest *Mabinogion* manuscript.
1250	Darkness of clairvoyant vision

SELECTIVE INDEX